SALES LAB SCRIPTING

SALES LAB SCRIPTING

THE PROVEN PLAYBOOK TO
SCIENTIFICALLY CRUSH YOUR SALES GOALS

BUTCH HODSON   A.J. MAHAR

))) Sellfire

SALES LAB SCRIPTING
The Proven Playbook to Scientifically Crush Your Sales Goals

FIRST EDITION

ISBN		
	978-1-5445-4782-4	*Hardcover*
	978-1-5445-4781-7	*Paperback*
	978-1-5445-4783-1	*Ebook*
	978-1-5445-4780-0	*Audiobook*

A.J. Dedication

To my parents, Alan Sr. and Cindy; my sister, Tana; my niece, Sadie; my grandmother, Sandy (Grammy); and the rest of my friends and family (you know who you are). You have been my greatest inspiration and have shaped me into the person I am today. This book exists because of you. Thank you and I love you.

Butch Dedication

To my family—

To Tamera, my rock star wife and greatest source of strength. You showed me what love is, and I'm grateful to share this journey with you.

To my children, Laney, Ava, Memphis, and Oakley, who give my life meaning and purpose. Each of you have saved my life more than you will ever know.

To my parents, By and Barbie, who have shown me the value of hard work, loyalty, resilience, and standing up for what you believe in. Thank you for never losing belief in me.

And to my siblings, Jessica, Fre, and Derek, thank you for being the best to your little brother. Your love and support mean the world to me.

This book is for all of you.

Joint Dedication

To the warriors on the front lines of sales—

This book is dedicated to you, the relentless hustlers who grind every day, pushing through rejection, setbacks, and the constant demands of the job. Your resilience, determination, and grit are the lifeblood of every business. We wrote this for you, to support your journey and help sharpen the tools you need to succeed. Here's to your hard work, your passion, and the victories yet to come.

CONTENTS

FOREWORD

—DAVID RUBIN, 9X ENTREPRENEUR
& CO-FOUNDER OF SELLFIRE

I'll never forget the first time I heard about Butch Hodson. My head of training popped into my office and said, "We've got a kid in the class who says he's going to be our number one salesperson—and I believe him."

To be clear, bold claims from new hires were nothing new. With 150 salespeople on the team, I'd heard plenty of overconfident rookies before. But this was different—my head of training had never vouched for someone like that. I was intrigued.

When I sat down with Butch, I asked him, "What makes you so sure you'll be the best?" His answer wasn't the usual fluff about past successes or natural talent. He looked me straight in the eye and said, "I can't go home at night, look in the mirror, and know someone with the same leads and opportunities outperformed me. I won't let it happen. I'll do whatever it takes to be the best—not because I want to, but because I have to."

He wasn't kidding.

Butch crushed it right out of training, landing in the top five salespeople immediately and claiming the number one spot in his first full month. His work ethic was unmatched—first in the office every morning, studying top sales calls, and often the last to leave, still closing deals late into the night.

The numbers were staggering. In an industry where most reps averaged five sales a month, Butch was signing up *120 customers a month*—24 times the industry average. He was closing a deal after every 13 dials on average, a jaw-dropping feat for a cold-call, demo-based sales process.

Curious about his secret, I listened to dozens of his call recordings. What stood out was his *consistency*. Every call followed the same structure—same opening, same tone and cadence, same approach to presenting our product and handling objections. It wasn't luck; it was a repeatable system.

I pulled him aside and asked, "Do you think you can teach the rest of the company your process?"

He didn't hesitate. Butch and A.J. Mahar, who was the newly promoted sales manager, took nineteen salespeople under their wing in what became our first Sales Lab. They broke down every line of the script—explaining the psychology behind the words, the importance of tone, and the timing of every statement. Within sixty days, their results proved the new system was superior, and we rolled it out to the entire team. The impact was transformative. We built the highest-productivity salesforce in the industry, propelling us to become the largest SEO company in the US.

Butch and A.J.'s success didn't stop there. Butch became the only frontline salesperson in our history to rise to VP, and A.J., as the person who understood the nuances of this new philosophy the best, became our head of sales performance. They subsequently took the new philosophy and process to scale high-performing sales teams at Yodle, Main Street Hub, and beyond. Over the decades, their scripting methodology has driven remarkable results across hundreds of industries and a wide variety of products and sales cycles.

Now, with *Sales Lab Scripting,* you're holding their proven playbook in your hands. Butch and A.J. are two of the best in the world at teaching the art and science of scripting for high-velocity sales teams. Follow their methods, apply their principles, and watch your sales soar!

INTRODUCTION

Let's get straight to the point: chances are you're reading this because you're not selling your product as well as you should be.

And if you're like most of the people we work with, the product isn't the problem. The problem is your sales process.

Don't worry; you're not alone.

Almost every team we coach has this problem. Most have one of the better products in their space, some solid marketing with a good flow of inbound traffic, and even some talented salespeople. The problem is they just don't have the sales numbers to back it up—or at least the sales numbers they want—and they don't know why.

We do.

In high-velocity sales (sales cycles of ninety days or less), there is a very specific playbook for maximizing sales revenue. Not just for individual salespeople but also for teams looking to scale their sales organization. And if you don't know that playbook, you're not only selling yourself short, you're selling your product and customers short as well. No pun intended.

The good news is we share that playbook in these pages. The

exact models, scripts, and strategies we've used to help dozens of startups scale and sell for hundreds of millions of dollars are contained in this book. Regardless of what industry you're in, experience you have, or product you sell, this system is scientifically proven to maximize revenue and scale your sales by 5x, 10x, or 100x.

When people ask us what we do for a living, the answer is simple: we teach a very specific kind of sales method, and we do it better than anyone on the planet. Now we're going to teach it to you.

NOT ANOTHER SALES BOOK

Have you ever read a book on "sales" before? Sure you have. After reading it, did your sales suddenly skyrocket so fast you never looked back?

Our guess is no. That's because most sales books suck when it comes to providing meaningful advice you can tactically apply to your own unique business model or role. They might get you pumped up for a day, a week, or a month, but they don't dramatically increase your sales every year like they say they will. They fall short on actual implementation. Why is that?

If you search "best sales books of all time" and read every book on the list, you'll see a pattern form: whatever the book's main theme (ask the right questions, challenge customers' beliefs, negotiation 101, outwork your competition, mindset for sales, etc.), they all contain broad guidance that can be applied to any sales role—outside sales, inside sales, quick sales cycles, long sales cycles, car sales, phone sales, enterprise sales, trade shows, and even door-to-door sales. The concepts in these books all sound great, but when you actually sit down and read them, you realize all they provide is generic, one-size-fits-all advice.

They're heavy on theory but light on practical application. They're more like motivational "self-help" books than manuals that teach you what to say and do for your exact product, role, and industry. Of course, this approach is great for the author's book sales. The broader their audience, the more books they can sell. But is it great for *your* sales? Can you apply their method today and see your sales graph spike tomorrow? Will it keep working reliably and predictably month after month? Nope, which is why you keep looking.

If your product requires a longer sales cycle (six to twelve months or more), you need to master a totally different set of sales skills and have a totally different company set up than if your product has a high-velocity sales cycle (days or weeks to make the sale). Making sales by phone relies on a completely different set of sales techniques than sales made in the field. And so on. So while general lessons on the principles of selling are helpful to keep in mind, they aren't tactical or, more important, applicable. They aren't going to tell you exactly what to say to a gatekeeper to gain access to the decision maker. They aren't going to teach you the specific things you need to show your sales prospect to convince them to close on the spot. And, if you're in management, they aren't going to give you the exact playbook to train and scale your sales team while increasing revenue per rep per day.

You need step-by-step advice on exactly what to say, how to say it, and when. That's why we wrote *Sales Lab Scripting*—to provide you real-life scripts and scientifically proven techniques you can start using immediately. Whether you're a brand-new sales development representative (SDR) setting appointments for your first job or a five-time CEO looking to scale your sales team, we want to share the exact playbook we've been using to help people just like you.

But first, it's important we be very clear about whom this book is for and whom this book is *not* for.

IS THIS BOOK FOR YOU?

Sales Lab Scripting is for any CEO, founder, executive, sales leader, sales rep, or SDR who has a product that can be sold virtually or over the phone in a high-velocity sales cycle—meaning there is less than three months from first contact to closing the sale, usually much less (within days or even same day). Although many of the techniques we share can be applied to other types of sales, this book is not designed for the outside sales professional (car sales, trade show reps, door-to-door sales, etc.), nor is it designed for the sales professional with a multimillion-dollar product and complex and lengthy sales cycle (three to twelve months or more).

Some of you might think you have a longer sales cycle, when in reality, you don't; you're just doing it wrong.

It's also worth noting that although this book reads as if we're speaking to a CEO or head of sales, we wrote it for the benefit of everyone in the sales organization. In fact, the first five chapters (out of eight) are dedicated to real-life scripts and strategies individual sales reps and managers can use on the phone to start seeing results immediately. The final three chapters are for the reader looking to scale their teams on this new process. Wherever you are in your company's org chart, we urge you to share this book with the people above you, below you, and on each side. Among all the companies we've worked with, the organizations that perform the best are the ones where everyone understands the system and is on the same page. Whether the message goes from the top down or the bottom up, the results of the system speak for themselves.

WHY LISTEN TO US

In 2009, we—Butch and A.J.—started working for a tech company in Austin, Texas, selling online advertising to small-business owners. It was a quick pitch, where we would cold-call the business owner. No inbound inquiries, no presentations or shared screens, just a completely blind call and an effort to close the sale by the end of that call. Needless to say, this was not the easiest job in the world. Especially with just a $12,000 per year base salary. If you didn't close, you didn't survive.

One of us (A.J.) was good at this and always one of the top sales reps. But Butch was on another level. He broke almost every sales record the company ever had.

At this company, top performers closed one sale out of every fifty dials. The average rep was making one sale out of every three-hundred-plus dials. Butch was one in thirteen. Now, if you know anything about cold-calling and high-velocity phone sales, you know how unheard of that is.

These types of results piqued the interest of the company's then-CEO—David Rubin, who wrote the foreword of this book. He asked Butch how it was possible he was having such success. Butch responded, "It's easy: I pitch everyone the exact same way." He had spent hundreds of hours studying calls, deliberately testing and practicing his pitch. He also mentioned that doing something the same way many times gave him the ability to refine what worked and what didn't.

Butch went on to tell David he could write a script and train anyone in the company to use his process, and they would instantly see results. David didn't think that was possible—they had tried prewritten scripts in the past, and they never worked. That being said, Butch's confidence convinced David to let him try.

Butch asked for a small team of reps and predicted that regardless of experience, personality, or performance rankings, his team would beat the seasoned sales reps and high performers. The only requirements were that the reps volunteered, were coachable, worked hard, had positive attitudes, and stayed on script. If they matched that profile, he knew they wouldn't fail.

He ended up with nineteen reps on his team (including A.J., who was to be the next manager promoted as long as he performed well on the test script). The team agreed to stay on process and be coachable. This was the infamous Team 19 trained by Butch in November 2010. By December, all of them had doubled, tripled, or quadrupled their sales (or more). Butch was promoted to sales director, A.J. was promoted to manager, and by January, the whole sales floor of more than 150 reps was using the new process. Even the top performers achieved 60 to 70 percent increases in sales in the very first month. The company went on a six-month tear of continuous record-breaking performance while also hiring twenty-plus new salespeople each month. Scaling suddenly became a lot easier with a playbook to get new hires selling right away.

These results caught the attention of a larger company that eventually purchased the company where Butch and A.J. worked. After the merger, Butch told the founders of the new company (John Berkowitz and Ben Rubenstein, both of whom wrote testimonials for this book) that he could do the same thing for them he had done for the previous company. Just as David had been skeptical, so were they. They thought because their product was more expensive and robust, there was no way Butch could pull off sales of that magnitude.

Butch temporarily stepped down as director of sales and went back to the phones to figure out how to adapt his sales playbook to the new company's products. Butch elected A.J. (who was a big help the first time around and understood his sales philosophies) to assist him. Within three weeks of getting on the phone, Butch was closing deals left and right, and he put up more commissionable revenue in that period than any of the other four-hundred-plus reps at the company.

Management was still skeptical Butch's system could work with hundreds of reps spread across five different offices. We traveled all over the country training each office on the new script and presentation, and in less than three months, all four hundred reps were using the new process. As the reps started onboarding the new system, we saw over 50 percent improvement in revenue per rep per day. The CEO called it the greatest sales improvement he had seen in his career.

The company launched a brand-new department called Sales Performance, which focused on scalable script creation, call coaching, training and management consulting, and, as the name suggests, overall sales performance. Butch was promoted to VP of Sales Performance, and A.J. was promoted to director of Sales Performance. We spent the next year collaborating every day and traveling to the company's different offices all over the US to boost performance. We even went to Canada for white-label partnerships.

In 2013, the company we worked for acquired another startup. This one sold CRM software for dentists—a totally new sales cycle, price point, prospect, and product for us. At the time of the acquisition, the dental CRM company had been in business for six years and just over a thousand dental practices were paying a monthly subscription to use its software. They had generated all their prospects through warm leads via marketing and had three inbound sales reps handling those leads. The CRM company's founder told us that, for many reasons, you can't successfully cold-call dentists. They had tried for years and hadn't been successful.

The short version of what happened next is Butch went to work figuring out how to make cold sales calls to dentists and how to close them in a short/high-velocity sales cycle. He signed up a large number of dental practices in the very first month with cold-calling. We worked together to polish the scripts and started training reps on the new outbound process. In less than three years, the dental CRM company went from three inbound reps to 120 outbound reps and one thousand customers to fifteen thousand. That kind of growth can propel an eight-figure business into nine figures.

Then A.J. took over sales performance for a different product, and management asked him to temporarily relocate to the island of Saint Lucia in the Caribbean. They wanted to know whether they could sell a US product to a US prospect from a call center in the Caribbean, which is less expensive to operate than one located in the US. Despite the heavy accents of the callers and substantial cultural differences, A.J. and the Saint Lucia team saw the same success that had followed each previous test of our system and even beat out some US-based teams just by sticking to the script.

THE BEGINNING OF SALES LAB SCRIPTING

We've helped scale multiple companies from one sales rep to teams of two hundred or more. We've assisted multiple startups in getting acquired through fast growth and healthy revenue streams. Our system works with great performers, low performers, inbound and outbound reps, and reps who are green as grass. We've even seen our process work in other languages and cultures. Each company we worked with was able to crush its sales goals, scale its sales team, and get acquired or exit.

Which is why we wrote this book. Our system works regardless of your industry, product, role, experience, or company's stage. We wanted to put our system down on paper and share it with everyone who is ready.

WHAT YOU'LL LEARN

Unlike books that take sixty pages to get to the point and provide something of real value to the reader, we're going to give you the actionable stuff right up front. Chapter 1 lays out some fundamental principles of how our system works. Chapter 2 shows you how to effectively cold-call by maneuvering past a gatekeeper, getting to the decision maker, and quickly convincing them to set an appointment with you by using confidence-building statements. Chapter 3 walks you through exactly how a product demo should be set up, how it should look, and what it should say. Chapters 2 and 3 include sample script templates that tell you what to say and how and explain why you're saying it. Chapter 4 demonstrates closing techniques to help you overcome a prospect's objections and get the sale. Chapter 5 teaches you how to research and test your product's strongest points and incorporate that information into your scripts. Chapter 6 covers assembling a team to test and refine your script, and Chapter 7 shows you how to roll the completed script out to your whole sales floor. Finally, Chapter 8 discusses important points about the management of a scripted team.

WHAT THIS BOOK CAN DO

When most people think about what a good sales system can do for their company, they only think about the individual sales rep or sales team. Sure, our system can help a sales rep learn fast, perform consistently, and make more sales. It can also help managers and trainers coach and scale their teams more effectively. But what can our system deliver for a company beyond just sales results?

Sales scripts done right can benefit everyone involved with your company—from the individual rep on the floor to the customer, customer service team, upper management, finance team, and even investors. Scripts help ensure consistent and correct product messaging and that every prospect receives accurate information about what your company offers. That makes for happy customers (and reduces risk). Happy customers stick around, which makes customer service happy. You also have more flexibility in hiring because you don't need to rely on sales outliers to carry your team. All of this helps with company culture. And for the C-suite, scripts deliver accelerated growth, predictably scalable revenue, and high customer and sales rep retention. High, predictable revenue and low, predictable customer churn make for happy investors.

If you commit to our system and follow it *exactly*, you'll see immediate results. You'll streamline your sales process with a clear, easy-to-follow structure. You'll build confidence in your sales team and sales leaders. You'll turn selling your product from a constant headache into the lifeblood of your business.

So let's get started and explain how scripting actually works.

CHAPTER 1

BUILDING THE RIGHT SALES SCRIPT

In this chapter, we'll give you a high-level look at our system, philosophies, and the basics of how to use and think about our call scripts. This will include:

- Correcting common misconceptions about scripting
- The three pillars to a good, scalable sales script
- The basic two-call structure
- How to deliver the script correctly
- Being a ninja versus a samurai
- Whom you should and should not be selling to

Scripted sales get a bad rap. This is probably because 99 percent of sales scripts are, in fact, bad. And that's because, typically, scripts aren't written by the right person or in the right way. Sometimes people have negative ideas about scripts because they don't understand the art of using one. They worry about sounding stilted, like a robot or someone simply reading aloud, and not having any creative freedom in the way they pitch a prospect.

All these misconceptions come from the same core misunderstanding of what's required to create and teach an effective and repeatable sales script.

Most of the time, the person writing the script doesn't have the perspective or experience to craft an effective, scalable pitch. It might be a manager whose unique approach won't work for anyone else. It might be a trainer who has never actually sold the product at a high level (or at all!). Worse yet, it might be a committee of trainers and sales managers who all want to show off their personal styles, creating a Frankenstein's monster of sales styles that barely makes sense.

Sometimes, a company's management will interview their highest-performing rockstar sales rep, write down what they say, and tell all the other reps to copy them. That almost never works. Outliers naturally gifted at sales work by intuition and charisma. They automatically change their approach based on what the prospect is saying in the moment, so their pitches are almost never the same twice, which makes them impossible to replicate.

Then, when the scripts don't work, they lose credibility, and managers give everyone a pass on actually following them. Reps go off script: they take the scripts as a guideline, put the pitches in their own words, and deliver them their own way. Just like the rock stars, they never deliver the same pitch twice, and they don't know why something worked or didn't. But of course, most reps don't have the intuition and charisma to sell on pure talent. So they struggle.

Managers want to help struggling reps, but if they don't know what the rep is saying and understand the importance of staying on script (or they don't have a good script in the first place), they will give subjective, vague, and, oftentimes, contradictory feedback. Without a clear playbook for training and coaching their reps, managers have nothing to offer but vague motivational speeches.

This happened to Butch on his first phone sales job. Sales leaders would walk around the cubes and encourage the reps. Occasionally, they'd stop by Butch's cubicle and say something like "Hey, let's get things going. We need two sales from you today."

Most of the reps would respond with "All right! You got it! Let's go!" But not Butch. He just got mad, and every time the leaders came around to say he needed to get more sales, Butch got more irritated.

One day, a leader came by and said, "Hey Butch, you didn't get a sale yesterday, so I need three from you today."

This time, Butch couldn't bite his tongue. He said, "Well, do you know why I didn't get a sale yesterday?"

The sales leader was confused. "What do you mean?"

Butch told him, "If you haven't listened to my calls and you don't know what I did wrong yesterday, how are you going to help me get three sales today? What am I supposed to do differently? Because if you can't tell me that, saying I need to get three sales doesn't help me at all."

What would have helped was sitting down to listen to calls and breaking down together what worked and why. That's the kind of detailed teaching we're going to do with you.

When you understand what works and why, you can write a script that will help any sales rep on your floor. With a well-written script, a brand-new hire can jump on a call and make a sale on their first day. Reps usually fear not knowing what to say or saying the wrong thing. They're a lot more confident when they know exactly what to say and how to say it. When managers know where a rep is in the script or where they went off script, they can better coach them, provide specific and actionable feedback, and see results. Additionally, a manager can jump on a call at the end and help the rep close because they already know what has been discussed and can just pick up where the rep left off.

METICULOUS SCRIPTING

It all starts with the why behind the words and the team understanding the theories and principles the script is built on. That's the key.

In a properly researched and written script, every word and sentence serves a purpose. Saying something the wrong way, paraphrasing, or leaving a sentence (or even a single word) out can change the meaning of the conversation and lose the sale.

You can have the best script in the world, but if no one in management holds their agents accountable to staying on that script, your results will tank. If your scripts aren't written precisely, taught thoroughly, and followed consistently, they're ultimately useless. As a matter of fact, it's pretty common for a rep to see their sales jump up by a huge margin when they start using our scripts, and then after a couple months, their performance declines. That's because at first, they're very careful to read the script word for word and deliver it the way it was intended. But after a while, they start to get comfortable or bored. They memorize the script (or *think* they memorized it), and then they start paraphrasing, summarizing, or saying the script in their own words. They skip phrases or sentences and ultimately stop making all the points contained in the original script. In essence, the script didn't stop working—they stopped working the script.

That's why we're going to discuss training and coaching in Chapters 6 and 7. Reps will see success when they get on script, but in order to keep succeeding, they have to *stay* on script and understand the whys behind the ways, and their managers need to hold them to it.

NO ROBOTS, PLEASE

Some reps are leery of being scripted, especially when they hear they'll have to stay on script word for word. They're afraid they'll sound like boring robots.

Nothing could be further from the truth. In addition to following the script, the salesperson has to use their active listening skills and be responsive to the prospect. After all, the prospect isn't using a script. They are spontaneous, so they interrupt, derail, and throw out objections you weren't anticipating. At that point, staying on script becomes an art form. You have to address what has come up and then get the conversation back on path. It takes a lot of practice, creativity, and interpersonal skills to do that, which are often overlooked skills in scripted sales.

In those moments, a well-crafted script is like having GPS in your car. When you're on a road trip, you have a precise route planned out to get to your destination. But suddenly, you encounter a five-car pileup on the freeway. If you try to keep going straight ahead, you'll crash. If you try to wait it out, you'll be stuck there and never arrive. You need to exercise good judgment to decide how to navigate around the obstacle and then resume your journey.

A good script gives you multiple off- and on-ramps to deal with prospect objections, but an effective rep still needs to be a really good listener. They need to understand which rebuttals to use when, how to cater rebuttals to the prospect, and when and how to get back on script. That is an art in and of itself. Our system gives reps the tools to be successful. They still have to assess the situation, choose the right tool, and use it correctly.

The biggest misconception about scripting is that everything is done for you—all you have to do is read the magic words and you'll get a sale. That's just not how it works! If that were true, you could hire high school students for minimum wage and still have a high sales volume. Our process makes reps more consistent, more confident, and much more successful. However, reps need many complex skills to use scripts correctly. Fortunately, all these skills can be taught. We've turned brand-new hires with zero sales experience and no natural sales ability into president's club award winners in their first year. Let's look at what makes a good, scalable script for new hires or reps with no sales experience.

THE THREE PILLARS OF A SUCCESSFUL, SCALABLE SALES PITCH

Our definition of a good script is one you can consistently train a team of brand-new hires or inexperienced reps on and in ninety days of repetition on the script, the vast majority of them are selling as if they were top performers.

To accomplish this, your sales pitch must contain three elements. It must (1) be **effective**, (2) be **efficient**, and (3) be **repeatable**. If it doesn't contain all three elements, you don't have a good, scalable pitch. Let's break each of these elements down.

#1—**An effective pitch** closes deals consistently. It should turn a "no" or "maybe" into a "yes" at a high rate. If it doesn't, the pitch needs to be more persuasive.

#2—**An efficient pitch** is a pitch that can close a prospect in as short a period of time as possible while also maintaining its effectiveness (a.k.a. high close rate). A good rule of thumb is if your pitch takes weeks or months to close a deal instead of days, the juice is probably not worth the squeeze, and you need a quicker, more efficient pitch.

#3—**A repeatable pitch** is a pitch that can not only be sold by a majority of the reps on your floor but can also be sold to a majority of the prospects you speak to. This is the tricky part. If your pitch is written so only the most advanced salespeople can understand and utilize it, it's not going to help an inexperienced new hire or scaling company flourish. The same is true for a pitch that only works on one specific type of prospect or personality. You need a universal pitch that can be applied to the vast majority of prospects and consistently repeated by the vast majority of sales reps on your floor—including new hires and inexperienced sales reps. If your pitch can't do that, you need a new pitch. Remember this: a script that closes at a 40 percent close rate by 80 percent of a sales floor will make four and a half times more profit than a script that closes at 70 percent by only 10 percent of the floor. We'll take the 40 percent close rate with four and a half times more revenue any day.

THE TWO-CALL APPROACH

Most companies we've worked with that have a high-velocity product to sell (SaaS, lead services, marketing companies, etc.) don't have an agreed-upon number of calls it should take to make a sale. We've tested every approach, and what we've proven time and time again is that regardless of the product, price point, or industry, the most effective and efficient approach is to set up your pitch to make a sale in just two calls.

Now, we know not all sales will happen perfectly in just two calls. This doesn't mean it will only take two calls to make a sale. We understand there will be callbacks, reschedules, and the like, but we set up the call structure to make the sale in just those two calls and do everything we can to close with that approach. Let's look at each call and its purpose.

During **Call 1**, the rep has two goals:

1. Set a demo: Schedule an appointment to present the product and its value propositions to a decision maker.
2. Collect key information about the prospect to personalize the product demo and close them on that next call.

This call should be very brief, so every word counts. We'll show you how this call script works in Chapter 2.

During **Call 2**, the rep presents a detailed product demonstration. This call will be much longer, but every word and visual is crafted to showcase the product and excite the decision maker enough to purchase.

You must understand the two calls have different goals and keep them separate. The goal of Call 1 isn't to get prospects excited about the product but to get them excited about the demo. A rep who wastes time overselling and giving too much information on Call 1 will get more objections and rejection as a result. It will hurt them more than it helps.

If the sales rep doesn't collect the right information during Call 1, they won't be prepared to address objections in Call 2, and that will throw them off course. The scripts for each call are crafted for their specific purpose so the rep is saying exactly the right things at the right moment and using their time as efficiently and effectively as possible.

Before we get to exactly what to say on Call 1, we need to

discuss something equally important to what you say: how you say it.

MORE THAN WORDS

When you have a great, scalable sales script, the reps need to use it word for word. But there's more to a script than just the words on the page. In order for your reps to deliver the script properly and say *what* they are supposed to say, they need to understand *why* each element of the script is there and how to deliver each sentence. Each section of our template scripts in Chapters 2 and 3 is broken down to include not just what to say but why and how to say it. Every element of the script is based on sales philosophies and techniques that govern the order, structure, and approach we use. Knowing why we included each phrase will help you add your product information effectively and deliver your messages confidently and sincerely. And being conscious of how you deliver the script will maximize your results. We call this "tonality."

HOW YOU SAY IT MATTERS

Tonality generally refers to your delivery, speed, pace, and sound of voice. But in the context of sales scripting, it's a much larger concept. It describes everything about the impression you make. Tonality is the feeling you give the prospect on the other end of the phone.

Since the prospect can't see you over the phone, nonverbal information comes through in your voice and manner of speaking. When you're speaking, the prospect is creating a picture of you in their head built on the way you sound. Like it or not, your potential customers are making judgments about you based on the way you speak that will make or break your sales pitch. So if you're not currently paying attention to how you sound, you should start.

We'll get into the details of tonality in the next chapter, but an example we like to use in training is that every time a prospect answers your phone call, you need to think of yourself as an actor auditioning for a movie role. The prospect is the casting director, and you need to convince them you're a super sharp expert consultant in your industry. This role will often require you to speak differently than you normally do. And if you don't read the script with that mindset, you won't get the role and you won't get the sale.

Ninja versus Samurai

If you surveyed most people and asked them what first comes to mind when they think of the word "salesperson," do you think those reactions would be mainly positive or negative? Unfortunately, with the way the media portrays salespeople, they would probably be mostly negative. Here are a few of the things you would hear:

- Pushy
- Deceptive
- Just in it for a sale
- Intrusive
- High pressure
- Lack of authenticity
- Rude

Let's break this down. The word "salesperson" conjures the mental image of a person whose end goal is to get a sale.

The means by which they achieve that goal is what gets a bad rap. For many years, we have been on a mission to change this perception.

We liken it to being a ninja versus being a samurai. When you're a ninja, your opposition never sees you coming. Think of the prospect as having a radar for salespeople. If their radar detects you're just a salesperson trying to make a sale, you lose your credibility. So you want to be hidden and off their radar. They won't see you as a salesperson; they will just see a professional who knows their industry and thinks the same way they do. If you take the time to anticipate objections and address them proactively, you can avoid potential conflicts and build trust with your prospect. In contrast, reactive objection handling is like being a samurai. You're attacking your enemy head-on, and you're forced to deal with objections in the moment, potentially putting the sale at risk. Thinking like a ninja is essential to our sales philosophy, and we use it throughout our scripts and this book.

All that being said, no matter how great your scripts and tonality are, or how much of a ninja you are, there are some prospects who will never set a demo with you or let you sell to them. Let's look at who they are.

UNDERSTANDING YOUR SALES PROSPECTS

Cold-calling can be challenging, and before a sales rep gets on the phone, they should understand not everyone is going to set an appointment with them. Understanding this and being prepared for the ways prospects differ will give them a psychological advantage and help them navigate their scripts appropriately. In phone sales, there are three different types of prospects: A Prospects, F Prospects, and B Prospects.

A Prospects

The A Prospect is very easygoing, sometimes referred to as a "lay-down." These are rare—a rep may only encounter an A Prospect 1 percent of the time while cold-calling. The minute a rep mentions the solution they're offering, the prospect says, "I was just looking for that exact thing! This is perfect for me!" They've been thinking about making this purchase for a while. They're eager to see the demo. They sign up immediately. They're already sold—the rep is just taking the order.

If your business depends on selling to A Prospects, it won't be very successful because they just don't come around too often. Finding them is pure luck. They are naturally occurring; you can't convert them. The only way to get more A Prospects is to dial more. Disclaimer: it is possible to screw it up with an A Prospect. Being off script is one way.

F Prospects

By contrast, F Prospects are predisposed against your product or being sold to at all. They're the type who hate salespeople. As soon as they figure out they're involved in a sales call, no matter what the product is, how good a deal it could be, what kind of script is used, or how great a salesperson is on the phone, the F Prospect is going to be near impossible to sell. The "F" in "F Prospect" represents the worst grade in school, but you can also think of it as standing for "friction," "fight," or "freaking bad prospects." (Or the kind of person who tells reps to F-off!)

A rep will encounter F Prospects much more often than A Prospects. They show up anywhere from 10 to 20 percent of the time. The F Prospect wants nothing to do with you. They don't care who you are or what you have to say. They don't believe in what you're doing and will challenge and fight you every step of the way. They may be rude and unprofessional or even yell and curse at you. It's essential that reps are mentally prepared for the reality of F Prospects because it is inevitable they will encounter some, and it can be a grueling experience.

On a day of cold-calling, a very good rep is likely to get rejected (politely or impolitely) more often than not. Most people just aren't built to deal with that volume of rejection. It can take a toll on a rep mentally, particularly when it involves insults and verbal abuse. Getting a "No thank you" or hung up on is mild by comparison. Being called a scammer, being screamed at, over and over? It's crushing.

Sales reps struggle with F Prospects because they want to sell their products and services to everyone. That's not realistic, and frankly, it's not healthy for the rep or the business to believe that's going to happen.

It is possible to sell to F Prospects—occasionally. We've done it—pitched and fought and ground the customer down until they finally say, "Screw it, I'll try it." But the amount of time and effort that goes into selling to an F Prospect just isn't worth it. If they are that awful to deal with in the sales process, just imagine what happens when they sign up. You've just handed an F Prospect on a silver platter to your customer service department to make their lives miserable. They'll never be happy—history shows that F Prospects rarely stay, no matter how hard you bend over backward trying to please them. In a month or two, they'll cancel. Then they'll leave bad reviews and bad-mouth you to anyone who'll listen. Reps should be cautious about not wasting time talking to F Prospects. Just let them go, and dial the next number.

One of the reasons cold-calling has such a stigma as the worst possible type of sales work is that most trainers and reps don't understand how to recognize F Prospects and why avoiding them makes sense for the business, the sales rep's morale, and the rep's personal bottom line. Reps can avoid wasted time and aggravation by not taking F Prospects personally and spending as little time as possible with them.

B Prospects

The vast majority of prospects aren't lay-down A types or hostile F types. They're somewhere in the middle, and those are the prospects our scripts are built for and who the reps should be focusing on. These are called "B Prospects." B Prospects will allow you to introduce yourself. They'll allow you to pitch to them. B Prospects will listen to you.

They might give you some objections and then set a demo with you. They might keep the appointment and let you deliver your entire presentation. But at the very end, they'll have a reason why they aren't going to buy from you right now. They're reasonable people with reasonable objections. They need to think about it. They need to do more research, talk to a partner or advisor, or look at their competitors.

We write scripts and train reps to focus on B Prospects because with a B Prospect, you have the chance to turn a no into a yes. You can turn "I want to think about it" into "This makes too much sense; let's do it."

Bear in mind, every B Prospect isn't going to set an appointment or buy. But when you look at your total list of leads, probably six or seven out of ten *could* set an appointment. You still have to earn their business, and a poor script or poor execution can turn a B Prospect into an F Prospect.

PUTTING IT ALL TOGETHER

Understanding the importance of staying *exactly* on script, remembering the goals of the two-call structure, and mastering the different aspects of tonality are necessary high-level concepts for selling to B Prospects. Now let's get granular and look at the structure and wording of your first call script.

A word of caution: these next few chapters go into *extreme* detail. Why? Because that's what moves the needle. We promise this book is unlike any other sales book you've ever read, so if you're not used to deep, meticulous detail, these next three chapters may take some time to get used to. You may need to reread sections multiple times. Buckle up—because this is where the money is made.

CALL NUMBER 1: MAKING THE PITCH

There are two types of leads. Warm leads—leads who have already inquired about your product or service—and cold leads—leads who have not yet inquired about your product or service. Each requires different scripting for Call 1—especially the introduction—which we'll detail throughout this chapter. Let's start with the harder of the two: cold leads.

The cold-call script has three (sometimes four) stages:

1. Managing gatekeepers (if required)
2. The intro
3. The "thirty-second" pitch
4. Setting the demo

This call is brief, but there is a **lot** going on in every line. We move fast and get right to the point because we're doing high-velocity sales. Relational selling requires a slow buildup of rapport, a personal connection with the prospect, and many points of contact. That's not effective or necessary for high-velocity selling. We build rapport and credibility in a completely different way—through professionalism and respect for the prospect's time. We're friendly, but we aren't trying to be friends. We put value on the table immediately.

We're polite, of course. But it's not personal. The only common ground we need to find is the point where they see value in what we're saying. We show them we understand their needs—including the need to save time.

Let's look at each section in detail.

MANAGING GATEKEEPERS

Many business owners and decision makers have a gatekeeper to screen their calls and help manage their time. The last thing a rep wants to hear is "Let me get your name and number," but if they aren't prepared, that's what they'll get every time. There are a number of ninja (not samurai) techniques we use to encourage the gatekeeper to pass you through to the decision maker.

There are two scenarios when managing gatekeepers. In the first scenario, you know the decision maker's name and are asking for them directly. In the second scenario, you don't know their name and need to empower the gatekeeper to tell you.

SCENARIO ONE: YOU KNOW THE DECISION MAKER'S NAME

For the sake of this template, we'll pretend A.J. is the sales rep and Butch is the decision maker. In the most basic interaction, the rep has three lines:

> Gatekeeper: Hello?
>
> (1) Sales Rep: Hi, yes. Butch, please.
>
> Gatekeeper: Who's calling?
>
> (2) Sales Rep: Oh, sure. Just tell him it's A.J. Mahar. Thank you.
>
> Gatekeeper: Okay. What's this in regard to?
>
> (3) Sales Rep: Oh, sure. Just tell him it's A.J. with Sales Lab Scripting. Thanks.

Line 1: The Greeting

During your research phase, you'll discover the name of the person you need to speak with. For your initial greeting, use their first name only:

> Sales Rep: Hi, yes. Butch, please.

This is the way a friend, family member, or client caller would normally interact with an assistant. They're on a first-name basis with the decision maker, and they assume the assistant recognizes their voice. They sound familiar. That means you also need to use a casual, familiar tone, like you're calling a friend or family member at their place of work. You want to make it sound like Butch knows who you are. Why? Because a gatekeeper is a lot more likely to pass a friend or family member over to the decision maker than a complete stranger, let alone a salesperson.

Whatever you do, don't say:

> Sales Rep: Hi, is Butch Hodson available/there?

They'll say no, even when he is available. The gatekeeper's job is to screen calls, and this question raises all the red flags—the biggest red flag being that the decision maker is not expecting your call, hence why you have to ask if they are available. This means you probably don't know them or haven't spoken with them before.

As human beings, we have a primal response to strangers that makes us suspicious. If we're dealing with someone we know, we are more open and approachable. You want your greeting to flip that psychological switch from the default "stranger" setting to the "familiar" setting so they will be more relaxed and comfortable talking to you.

Without that implied familiarity, the gatekeeper will assume this is a sales call. Gatekeepers are wary of sales calls because their bosses are wary of sales calls. Business owners and decision makers get a lot of sales calls, maybe as often as every day. They have a lot to do, and they don't want to be interrupted. They need to earn money by dealing with their own clients, so they don't want to waste time. And the gatekeepers don't want to get in trouble for wasting their boss's time. Their resistance is high.

In sales terms, that's an "objection." You need to get past that mindset and create positive expectations that this is a call the boss will want to take. Of course, you never want to lie your way into a sales call—that's shady and will give your business a bad reputation. However, you do want to subliminally convey that you are a welcome caller, and using the decision maker's first name does just that. After all, the gatekeeper doesn't want to make a mistake by turning away someone the boss should be talking to.

Some gatekeepers are very friendly and eager to please. Once their "stranger danger" defenses are down, they'll pass you through to the decision maker, no questions asked. Some are on high alert all the time and won't let anyone through for any reason. Most are in the middle, and they might ask a question or two before they feel comfortable passing you on, so let's look at the next lines.

Line 2: The Power of "Just"

Sales Rep: Oh, sure. Just tell him it's A.J. Mahar. Thank you.

If a gatekeeper asks follow-up questions—like "Who's calling?" There's a very powerful word to use: "Just."

The subtext here is that the decision maker should know the rep's name and want to take the call. Inflection is key to conveying that subtext correctly. If the representative says, "Just tell her it's A.J." in a casual, friendly tone, it sounds like a perfectly normal interaction, as if you can take it for granted that the decision maker knows who you are. Try it and see.

If the rep says, "Just tell her it's A.J." in a completely flat or demanding inflection, that sounds like a threat. Instead of worrying about whether Butch knows you, the gatekeeper won't want to put you through because you sound like a jerk.

You can hear examples of correct tonality on our website, www.Sellfire.com/SalesLabScripting.

There are several factors in play here. You have the assumption your voice should be familiar. If you're a friend or family member to the decision maker, it shouldn't be a big deal to pass the phone over to them. "Salesperson" doesn't even come to mind. You are being very agreeable by saying, "Oh, sure."

Combined with the word "just," this implies the call is not a big deal and doubles down on the same message in your tonality that this is a routine interaction and shouldn't ping anyone's "stranger danger."

A good script uses these automatic social routines to your advantage. In a way, it short-circuits people's normal thought patterns. They go from thinking, "Who is this person? They sound like they know Butch, but I'm not sure who it is," to "Oh, they must know him. I'll pass him through."

The Conversation Ender

You then end the interaction by saying "Thank you." The phrase "thank you" is polite, but it's also a conversation ender. The implication is this little conversation is over, and you're expecting to move on.

A lot of our routine social interactions run on autopilot to a certain extent. We're programmed from childhood to respond in certain ways out of habit. When someone says "Thank you," it's almost a reflex to respond with "You're welcome." If the gatekeeper says that, they've acknowledged they're going to get the decision maker for you, or why else would they say "You're welcome"? It also implies the conversation is over now, so they think, "Okay, I'd better go get Butch."

It seems a bit abrupt at first, but if you use the power of "just" with the "conversation ender" correctly, it works more often than not. Once a gatekeeper has this new thought pattern, it makes it difficult for them to go back and try to interrogate you further.

Line 3: The Final Challenge

If you haven't been passed over yet, that means our gatekeeper in this example isn't quite so agreeable. Instead of saying, "You're welcome," this person is a little more difficult. This second round of questioning might include "Where are you calling from?" or "What's this regarding?"

Your reply should stay just as pleasant and personable while providing your name and your company's name.

> Sales Rep: Oh, sure. Just tell him it's A.J. with Sales Lab Scripting. Thanks.

Again, you're implying this should be enough information that the decision maker will recognize you and want to take the call.

If, for some reason, that doesn't work, don't mess around. Some sales books will recommend elaborate schemes to try to trick a gatekeeper into putting your call through. That's not going to do the rep or the business any good because it erases all the effort you put into creating a good impression. They have your name and the name of your company, and they think you sound shady. That's the opposite of what you want.

Instead, after the third try, it's time to change your approach. Now, instead of trying to make it easier on the gatekeeper to pass you through, you want to empower them to help in some way.

> Sales Rep: Okay, no problem. Butch might not be the best person to speak with here. Maybe you can help point me in the right direction. Who would I speak to that handles [XYZ]? Would that be you, or would that be someone else?

XYZ = any part of their company that your product could impact. For example, if your software handles patient communication for medical practices, you would say, "Whom would I speak to that handles patient communication and scheduling? Would that be you or someone else?"

Now, instead of being in a defensive position against the gatekeeper, you are aligned. They are helping you solve your problem. There are only two options in that question: themselves or someone else. Whichever answer they give, you're now on the same page.

SCENARIO TWO: YOU DON'T KNOW THE DECISION MAKER'S NAME

In the second type of gatekeeper situation, you don't know the name of the person you're trying to reach.

In that case, you'd use a very similar approach as when the gatekeeper keeps asking questions: you get them on your side by asking them for help.

> Gatekeeper: Hello?
>
> Sales Rep: Hi, yes, this is A.J. Mahar with Sales Lab Scripting. Maybe you can help point me in the right direction. Who handles [XYZ]? Would that be you or someone else?

This makes it easy on the gatekeeper to give you an answer without thinking. There are several different ways the conversation could go from here. You might wind up talking to a different decision maker. You might wind up leaving a voicemail. The gatekeeper might hang up on you. Each of these options has its own path to follow in a fully developed script.

CALLBACKS

There are going to be times when the decision maker is not available to take your call. A lawyer could be in court, or a business owner could be on vacation, and you won't ever know if the gatekeeper is telling the truth or not. Following our strategies is the best you can do to maximize your chances of getting to a decision maker in a legitimate way without doing shady or unethical things to get through. So there are going to be times when you have to call back, and that's okay. That's just part of the job.

If that's the case, let's prepare you for the things you need to know and get right before you introduce yourself and pitch to the decision maker.

FIRST IMPRESSIONS

In face-to-face sales, your first impression on the prospect comes from your appearance, demeanor, and body language. Like we mentioned in the previous chapter, on the phone, none of that physical or visual information comes across. Instead, you must focus on the mental image the prospect will instantly form of you upon hearing your voice. Like it or not, within about five seconds of speaking, the prospect will make assumptions about how old you are, what you look like, your intelligence, your credibility, and your professionalism just based on the first ten words that come out of your mouth. And if you don't say the right words in the right way from the start, it is extremely difficult to change that impression.

Being prepared is key to making a good first impression. Some reps lose an opportunity because they fall into the rut of dialing without expecting an answer. They put themselves on mute and mentally zone out or even browse the internet.

Then, when the prospect actually picks up, they fumble around, take too long, and sound nervous and unprepared. That's the equivalent of showing up late to a business meeting with your shirt untucked and coffee stains on your pants. So many sales get lost in the first couple seconds because the rep isn't immediately ready when the prospect says "Hello?"

Instead, you need to sit upright in your chair—script in front of you, fully prepared, ready to go—and not pause after the person answers the phone.

THE INTRO

Not all decision makers have gatekeepers. Many potential clients answer their own phones. If there's any reasonable chance the person who answers the phone might be your contact (like if you're calling for Butch and a male answers the phone), it's best to assume they are the decision maker and greet them by name. If it isn't actually Butch, they'll tell you, and you can use the gatekeeper script. Once you reach the decision maker, whether that's on the initial dial or after speaking to the gatekeeper, you need to get straight to the point with four things: who you are, why you're calling, what you do, and the quick pitch. We'll continue using A.J. as the rep and Butch as the decision maker.

> Prospect: Hello?
>
> (1) Sales Rep: Hi, Butch?
>
> Prospect: Uh, yes, this is he.
>
> (2) Sales Rep: Hey, Butch. This is A.J. Mahar with Sales Lab Scripting. Are you familiar with Sales Lab Scripting, Butch?
>
> Prospect: [Says yes or no. Both can receive the same reply.]
>
> (3) Sales Rep: Okay, yeah. I wasn't sure if maybe you had seen us in [relevant industry news]. By the way, Sales Lab Scripting, just really quickly, we [help growing businesses scale their sales team].
>
> (4) I know you're extremely busy right now, so why don't we do this: let me give you a quick thirty-second description of what we do, and if it interests you, we can always set up another time to talk. Sound good/is that fair?

The rep really only has four lines in this section, but they each have a lot of elements, so let's break it down one phrase at a time. Remember, these first few seconds are when pace and speed matter most.

LINES 1 AND 2: FAMILIARITY AND OBLIGATION

> Prospect: Hello?
>
> (1) Sales Rep: Hi, Butch?
>
> Prospect: Uh, yes, this is he.

Just as with a gatekeeper, you don't want to sound their "stranger danger" alarm. Like we just mentioned, the way you accomplish this is by always assuming the decision maker answered the phone. If the decision maker answers the phone and you say, "Hi, is this Butch?" you're subconsciously telling them you don't recognize their voice (and are therefore a stranger). Instead, as long as they don't state it's someone else, you should always use the prospect's first name, and your tone should imply you recognize their voice and they should recognize yours. It should have the same level of enthusiasm you would use if you were talking to a longtime business colleague you hadn't spoken with in a while.

In addition to flipping that instinctive switch from stranger to familiar, you are adding a layer of social obligation. We've all had experiences where we run into someone, and they know us, but we can't place them. It's awkward. We feel a little bit guilty. We don't want to be impolite. So those two little words—"Hi, Butch?"—delivered with the right tonality, carry a lot of psychological weight.

> (2) Sales Rep: Hey, Butch. This is A.J. Mahar with Sales Lab Scripting. Are you familiar with Sales Lab Scripting, Butch?
>
> Prospect: [Says yes or no. Both can receive the same reply.]

You don't stop there. The goal here is to get to the point as quickly as possible, so introduce yourself using your full name and the name of your company. There are a couple points to notice here.

First, you don't say, "My name is..." You say, "This is..." There's only one social circumstance when you'd normally say, "My name is..." It's when you're meeting someone for the very first time. That phrase puts you right back in the "stranger danger" zone. However, when you say, "This is..." in a friendly, familiar tone, you imply you might have met before, and your contact continues to wonder when and where.

Additionally, you use your full name because it makes you unique. It gives your name some importance. It lets them know you have nothing to hide. After all, scam artists tend not to give out their full names. Finally, you want to make sure you speak your name and company name slowly, confidently, and clearly, almost as if the person should recognize who you are and where you're calling from. This is where most reps speak too fast, sound nervous, and kill their first impression. But if delivered the right way, with confidence, this will set you up perfectly for the next part of your script, where you add on a key question: "Are you familiar with [company name]?"

Here's an important example of why every word matters. In this question, you ask "Are you familiar with us?" not "Are you familiar with us *by chance*?" You also avoid using any other phrase that casts doubt, like "maybe" or "happen to be" or "perhaps." Up to this point, we have been planting the idea in the prospect's mind that they *should* be familiar with us. Adding "by chance" or any equivalent completely negates that subtext. Those two seemingly innocuous words don't match the subtext of your pitch and can throw off the rest of the call and lose the sale.

That's how precise scripting needs to be. That's how precisely we train and how precise we want our reps to be.

Closed-Ended Questions

A strong sales script works like a flowchart: you ask a question, the prospect responds, and their reply dictates your next move. For that flowchart to work properly, you must give the prospect a limited number of options for their response. That means you should never ask open-ended questions, only closed questions. A rookie might start by saying:

> Sales Rep: Hey, my name is Joe calling from the Product People. How's it going today?

Right away, you have a problem. "How's it going?" could take you in eighteen different directions. Most likely, it's going to take the prospect right off the phone because they'll say they're busy and can't talk right now. They know you don't really care how their day is going; you're just saying it to get to the next part of the call. It's disingenuous, and you're wasting their time—two things you never want to do. You should only ask "How are you?" or "How's it going?" if you've met the person before and they're expecting your call.

Instead, you can direct them into a useful response by asking, "Are you familiar with us?" Now the prospect has a binary choice: yes or no. Either of those answers will allow you to continue your pitch because you'll have responses prepared for both. If they say no, it's no problem because you've already introduced yourself and you have a response prepared. If they say yes, your tonality probably worked and they didn't want to admit they don't know you to save face, and again, we have a response for that.

LINE 3: CREDIBILITY AND PURPOSE

> (3) Sales Rep: Okay, yeah. I wasn't sure if maybe you had seen us in [relevant industry news]. By the way, Sales Lab Scripting, just really quickly, we [help growing businesses scale their sales team].

When you ask whether the prospect has heard of you and then immediately mention a real place they might actually have heard of you, you build legitimacy in their mind. It's also a way of anticipating an objection and solving it immediately. Who wants to take a call from a random company nobody's heard of? You're planting the seed of an expectation that they might have heard of you. It also drops a hint that maybe they *should* know about your company. That adds some psychological leverage that they might be out of the loop.

In the second half of this line, you place a very, very brief summary of the product or service you offer. You'll create this statement during your research and development phase (which we'll talk about in Chapter 5), but this is where speed and pace are super important. By being quick and direct about the purpose of your call, the prospect knows this is a sales call and can see you're not beating around the bush. They don't have to guess at what you might be selling or wonder if you're playing mind games. Make sure you say these lines quickly so you don't get cut off with a "I'm busy right now; call me back"–type objection. At the same time, though, make sure you're very clear and confident in your speech. You want to sound as if you're an expert in their industry who is not there to waste time, not an amateur who is nervously rushing.

This line is said straight through, no pauses.

LINE 4: WITH PERMISSION

(4) Sales Rep: I know you're extremely busy right now, so why don't we do this: let me give you a quick thirty-second description of what we do, and if it interests you, we can always set up another time to talk. Sound good/is that fair?

At this point in the call, the prospect is aware it's a sales call, so we have a very brief window to get their permission to continue. You have to say this line quickly, without any pauses between the words. Being quick also matches the subtext of the line. It would sound counterintuitive to say "I know you're busy right now, so I'll be quick" in a slow-paced tone. It just doesn't match.

When we listen to calls, the sales reps who don't get out a lot of pitches on the cold call are almost always too slow here. If you keep getting cut off with "I'm busy right now" or "Call me back," even though you're saying the same thing as other reps, it's not because you have bad luck—it's because you haven't mastered your speed and pace.

As you can see, this short line is doing a lot of heavy lifting. You're anticipating their objection about being busy. You're making a promise to be quick and to give them a clear, logical reason for your call. You're also getting their permission to pitch to them. Thirty seconds is a very small amount of time to ask for, which makes it hard for them to say, "No, I don't have thirty seconds." Because they do. Everyone has thirty seconds.

We call this "time-stamping," and it's very important. Without it, you're asking the prospect to commit an unknown amount of time to hear you out. If you don't time-stamp, you'll get cut off a lot and told "Send me an email," "I don't have time right now," or "Not interested" because they don't want to sit through some long-winded sales pitch. Who knows? They might think this call is going to take an hour or that you might even try to sell them something at the end of the call. Without time-stamping, they jump to conclusions about your intentions. They want no part in making decisions that impact their business with a complete stranger over the phone. If your intentions are clear—you'll only take thirty seconds of their time and then let them go—they can't jump to those unhelpful conclusions. We want to proactively eliminate objections before they come up.

This is an example of something we call "proactive objection elimination," which we will explain in further detail when we discuss Call 2. Just remember it's much easier to overcome an objection by proactively addressing it in your script than to reactively handle it when a prospect brings it up. So the more proactive objection elimination you can do in your scripting, the better.

Finally, you ask, "Is that fair?" Here's another closed-ended question, and one that really only has one answer. Nobody wants to think of themselves as being unfair. They are getting a call from a salesperson who is only asking for thirty seconds and then will let them go. Is that really unfair compared to what they are used to? It is very difficult for someone to say, "No, I don't have thirty seconds," especially to someone who is being professional and getting straight to the point.

In some circumstances, you can proceed without asking for permission. We have taught it both ways successfully. It depends on the industry and type of prospect. Time-stamping and permission are more important on outbound cold calls and less commonly used on inbound calls. If a warm lead is reaching out to you with intent, you can jump into a pitch without asking for permission. They came to you, so you already have their permission.

However, on an outbound cold call, you absolutely need to time-stamp, whether you ask, "Is that fair?" or not. Jumping into a pitch without telling them it will only take thirty seconds puts you right back into the "Send me an email" or "Not interested" objections.

That would make Lines 3 and 4 look like:

(3) Sales Rep: Okay, yeah. I wasn't sure if maybe you had seen us in [relevant industry news]. By the way, Sales Lab Scripting, we [help growing businesses scale their sales team].

(4) Really quickly, though, I can give you pretty much a thirty-second rundown of what we do over here at Sales Lab Scripting, and if it interests you, we can set up another time to talk.

THE "THIRTY-SECOND" PITCH

Assuming they agree, you can begin transitioning into your pitch. We can't give you an exact template for your quick pitch because it is specific to your company and product and tailored to the needs and concerns of your prospects. The whole point of building your sales lab (as we discuss in Chapter 5) is to create, test, and refine this pitch. We can give you some guidelines, though.

ASKING QUESTIONS

Before you begin your pitch, slip in a question or two that will help you gain leverage on the prospect and allow you to throw in confidence-building statements about your product. Whatever the key benefits of your product may be, the questions you ask should help separate you from the competition and create leverage for how your product will help them run their business better than what they're currently doing—whether that's getting more leads, operating more efficiently, saving time so they can serve more clients, upgrading their offerings so they can charge more money, and so forth.

For example, a pre-pitch question might be:

Sales Rep: Which platform are you using right now for your scheduling? Is it [Company A] or [Company B]? **[GO INTO THIRTY-SECOND PITCH.]**

By name-dropping two well-known industry players, you show you understand the industry and add to your credibility. And if it's neither, they'll tell you which one they do use, which adds to your industry knowledge for future pitches. Other relevant questions could include asking about the size of their company, how many clients they deal with in a day or a week, and their most popular products or services. Some questions will help you decide which bullet points to present in your pitch. Some may reveal the prospect isn't a good fit for your product. Some will provide information you can use to counter the clients' objections later on. For example, they might tell you they have two hours a day they'd like to devote to new business, but at the end of the call, when you're asking for the demo appointment, they say they aren't interested, it's not a good fit, or they don't have time, and you can remind them they already acknowledged, earlier in the conversation, that they need new business.

Choose your questions carefully. You don't want to annoy the prospect or make them regret giving you permission to pitch.

The Body of the Pitch

Once you have your answers, you're ready to deliver your thirty-second pitch (which might take more than thirty seconds but should be quick and to the point). Now, how can you pitch a complex product in less than one minute? After all, a full product demo could take forty-five minutes to an hour, so how can you boil that down to thirty seconds (more or less) and still have it be meaningful? You have to remember that your goal on this call is *not* to sell the product. It's to set the demo appointment.

First, consider that a thirty-second pitch might not take *exactly* thirty seconds. Human beings don't inherently have an accurate sense of time. That's why we need watches and cell phones with timers. If you ask your prospect for thirty seconds and your pitch actually takes forty-five seconds or a minute, they aren't going to be sitting with a stopwatch to cut you off (or not often, anyway).

Every time we train new reps on our system, we do this exercise: We draw a clock on the whiteboard with the hands pointing to some random time and tell everyone to put away their phones and watches. We have them stare at the clock and wait. After five or ten minutes, we ask each person how long they waited.

The answers are always all over the map. Some people think it was three minutes. Some think it was ninety seconds; some think it was fifteen minutes. Some people's minds wander. Some try to count the seconds, but they never count precisely.

We don't recommend you spend five minutes on your pitch. Keep it brief and to the point—under two minutes is best. But as long as your pitch is relevant and engaging, the time will feel shorter than it is.

Just Specific Enough

The science of a thirty-second pitch is to be heavier on benefits and lighter on features—include just enough specifics to get them interested and make them want to hear more, but don't go into so much detail they find reasons to say no.

Let us explain with an analogy. You're hosting a Super Bowl party for a hundred people. You made your famous original dip, and your goal is to get as many guests as possible to try it. When you ask if someone wants to try your dip, most people want to know what kind of dip it is or what's in it. And a lot of people have ingredients they don't like.

Let's say one guest hates mayonnaise. If you start listing off the recipe and mention mayonnaise, they're immediately turned off. There might be such a small amount they'd never even notice, but as soon as you say the word "mayonnaise," they fixate on that one item, tune all the other ingredients out, and decide they don't want to try it.

Instead, you want to respond with a CBS: confidence-building statement. CBSs are going to be a main tactic in proactively handling objections throughout Call 1 and Call 2. In this example, your CBS would focus on relating the dip to something you already know the guest likes.

You might say, "I see you're drinking red wine. I made this dip especially to pair with red wine, and everyone who has tried it with red wine has loved it. In fact, last year, it won the award for best dip. You're going to thank me for this. It's going to be the best dip you've ever had."

Once they try it and like it, the mayonnaise won't matter anymore. You've got their buy-in. After they admit they love it, you can then give them the ingredients. It might change their opinion of mayo.

Your prospect hasn't had the opportunity to fully experience what the entire product is capable of. So if you just start listing features, any one of them might put the prospect off and make them feel the product isn't relevant for them. If you have twenty features in your product, eight or nine of them are probably applicable to every prospect, and the others are useful for some and not others. The point is to distill them down into a handful of benefits that anyone should be interested in.

SETTING THE DEMO

After delivering your thirty-second pitch, don't pause or stop. Don't ask the prospect what they think about what you've said so far. You aren't done, and you don't want them making any decisions yet.

When you finish the final bullet point of your pitch, immediately ask for an appointment:

> Sales Rep: So, why don't we do this? We don't have to take up any more of your time right now. Let's set up a time when you can be in front of a computer for fifteen or twenty minutes, and I will give you a quick product demo of what our platform does and how well it will integrate with everything you're currently doing. Does later today work, or tomorrow morning?

GET ON THE CALENDAR

Most product demos are going to take thirty to forty-five minutes. Some might take up to an hour. But most people run their calendar in and have a mental default to half-hour increments. They automatically assume they can't fit in an hour-long call. They also know most meetings run long, so if they agree to one hour, it might turn into two.

If you ask for fifteen or twenty minutes, they only need to find a thirty-minute window. And if you provide enough value during that demo, you will earn their buy-in for an extra fifteen or twenty minutes to finish the call.

It's also important that you ask to set a specific time. Don't leave it open-ended by saying, "When works best for you?" The prospect might respond with some time a week or two weeks away, or never. You might ask for tomorrow morning or afternoon—the point is it's a very short turnaround. You always want to give two options to make it easier for them to choose.

The prospect will either choose morning or afternoon, and it's better to ask what time works best for them in the morning. Their first response will give you the best chance they'll actually show up for the appointment. Some reps like to sound busier and more prestigious than they actually are, so they offer certain time slots or try to go back and forth negotiating a slot. That's a bad idea because a business owner doesn't care what's more convenient for a sales rep.

Whatever time they say works for them, book it. If you have another demo set for the exact same time, hand it off to another rep and split the commission. Setting the appointment doesn't guarantee the prospect will show, so anything you can do to increase the chances of them keeping that appointment is worthwhile. Don't worry about being double-booked. You can always choose to run the more valuable prospect and have your colleague run the other.

If the prospect turns it around and asks for time slots, you should never say you're wide open. Maybe you are, but it dings your credibility. A professional expert is busy and has to manage their time. So you should suggest a time and adjust from there.

It's also a way to demonstrate that you're a good listener and responding to the prospect's needs. Some people hate playing ping-pong with their calendar. If they ask you to provide a time slot, give them a specific answer.

Data show you get the best retention if you run the demo within three days or less of the initial call. Sometimes a prospect will say, "Call me in a couple weeks." That's not a good idea if you can avoid it. If they are going on a two-week vacation or are completely unavailable, the delay is unavoidable. But after the first week, chances drop off tremendously that the prospect will ever show up.

PERSONAL CONTACT

Once the prospect commits to a day and time, you need to get their personal contact information. That's usually the best email address to send the calendar invitation to. You also want to get a phone number. Asking for a prospect's cell number can feel intrusive because people worry about getting unsolicited calls. They're more likely to give out their main business line. We've found the easiest way is to ask for the best number to send text reminders to. Then we give out our contact information as well. That strengthens the professional connection. Here is an example:

> Sales Rep: Okay, great, and what's a good email to send the calendar invite to? Okay, and what's the best number to send a text reminder to for the appointment? Okay, perfect, and let me give you my phone number just in case you need to get in touch with me in the meantime.

Scheduling the Right People

At the end of your pitch, after you've delivered your key bullet points, it's important to ask whether there are any other decision makers who need to be on the call. This is a good example of the difference it can make to be on or off script by even a word or two.

Your goal is to discover whether they are the sole decision maker or they have a partner or boss who would need to approve a purchase. You should never ask:

Sales Rep: Is there anyone else who should be on the demo call?

If the person you are speaking with is gatekeeping someone else's time or if they want to use this second layer of approval as an "out" to defer a buying decision, they will automatically say no. They don't need the other person on the call because they will report back to them and ask their opinion behind the scenes. You want to avoid that step because it can delay the sales cycle. Not to mention you don't want decisions discussed without you there to possibly rebut any objections.

Instead, you should ask:

Sales Rep: If you love the product, is there anyone else involved in that approval process?

If they say yes, you need to schedule the demo when that second decision maker can join in. We present this as making it more efficient to run a single presentation instead of having to explain the value of the product to multiple people. Even if you have to schedule the demo a few days further out to get that second person on the call, it's worth it. If the prospect insists they will attend alone, you should go ahead and schedule. But it's worth making at least one attempt to get everyone who should be involved in the demo.

WRAP UP

There are just a few more steps to complete Call 1. We need to set their expectations for the importance of the demo, create psychological reinforcement that they will keep the appointment, and build anticipation about the product itself.

EXPECTATIONS

You need to ensure the prospect expects a high level of professionalism and value from the demo. They need to think of this appointment as something significant for their business that they don't want to miss. So explain that you will invest time and energy into preparing on your end: "Between now and our meeting time, I'll do more research on the business and get a better idea of your needs." Assure them you'll put together a great presentation that will show exactly how you can help their business.

Reinforcement

It's time to create a little pressure on the prospect. You have shown respect for their time by being brief and providing value. Now you ask them to respect your time in return.

> Sales Rep: If for any reason you are not able to make our appointment at [the meeting time], please personally call me and let me know. I'm investing a lot of time into putting together this presentation for you, so please give me the courtesy of a heads-up if you can't make it, and I'll do the same for you if anything comes up on my end. Is that fair?

There are a number of psychological levers working together here. First, you're asking for a call rather than an email or text message. You don't want to make it too easy for them to cancel, and you don't want to waste time. If they text or email to reschedule, you might make the mistake of texting back to ask for a good time. If the prospect doesn't reply, you could lose a whole week before the appointment gets reset. If you get a phone call, you get a chance to reschedule on the spot and address any underlying concerns or problems.

Sometimes there's a real conflict that comes up. More often, they have second thoughts and feel it's not the right time to look for new solutions or change their business process. If you're on the phone, you have the chance to overcome that objection, make them feel better about it, and get the demo rescheduled. If they just cancel by email, you might never talk with them again. They might cancel because they don't want the added pressure that comes with an upcoming sales presentation. You can't ease their minds if you aren't speaking with them.

Next, you're asking for courtesy. Most people want to be courteous. You've been very professional and polite. They feel a social obligation to be polite in return.

Finally, you restate the date and time of the appointment again. You've repeated it several times, as a matter of fact. This helps it stick in the prospect's mind. Of course, you'll also send a calendar invitation, but hearing it over and over gives it a sense of importance.

SDRs and AEs

Some sales teams split the tasks of setting appointments and running demos into two roles: sales development representative (SDR) and account executive (AE). This is a popular debate in many companies. Sometimes SDRs are very much needed. Other times, it's better for AEs to do everything themselves. It all depends on the setup and how they are coached.

On a split team, this stage of setting expectations and reinforcing the appointment will sound a little different but work very much the same way. An SDR would set expectations that a product expert will prepare and make the presentation. For software, it might help to include an engineer on the demo (or suggest that one might possibly attend). The SDR would use CBSs about how the account executive is one of their best people and emphasize they are handing the prospect over to a higher-level person at the company for white-glove treatment. They could even suggest the head of sales might attend.

Done right, booking the appointment can actually strengthen the sense of mutual relationship and obligation for the prospect to keep the appointment. The SDR can lean into the idea that it will reflect badly on them if the prospect is a no-show because they will have one or two very senior people booked on the demo call.

ANTICIPATION

You always want to end on a positive note. The last step may not be a completely new thought, but it should build anticipation without giving too much away. It could be as simple as a statement that you're excited for them to see the presentation and you think they'll love it. You might reiterate one or two of the bullet points from the pitch. You should certainly reiterate the appointment time.

Example:

Sales Rep: All right, great. So I have you scheduled for **[DAY and TIME]**. Again, I am **[FIRST NAME]** with **[COMPANY NAME]**, and I am really excited to show this to you. I think you're going to be really impressed, especially around **[FEATURE]**; you will absolutely love everything we are doing. All right, **[THEIR NAME]**, I will talk to you soon. Have a great rest of your day.

EXPECT OBSTACLES

Throughout this chapter, we've talked about the script as if there would be no pushback or objections. As much as we like our scripts and are confident in our approach, we know things won't always go that smoothly. One of the many reasons it is difficult to keep reps on script in the first place is because of their unrealistic expectations. If something doesn't work right away, reps typically want to bail and try something else. The reality is even if you have the best cold-call script in the world and you execute it perfectly, you are going to get objections, get hung up on, and fail way more often than you succeed.

For example (again, these numbers may vary based on your company and industry), if a rep makes one hundred dials in a day, they may actually only connect with someone 20 to 30 percent of the time. Of those twenty or thirty connections, they may only get the person they need to pitch to less than half the time. This leaves them in a scenario where a rep may actually only pitch ten to fifteen people a day. Of those ten to fifteen people, a solid day would result in two or three new demo sets. This means for a rep to be successful, they will fail a lot more than they will succeed. The key is to hold the course. Three new quality demo sets in a day is a good day for some companies, so reps need to remember that and trust the process. We emphasize "quality" because we don't want to just set a demo. We want to set a demo that the prospect is going to show up to and be excited about. That being said, what separates the top appointment setters from the rest of the sales floor is their ability to handle cold-call objections appropriately and quickly navigate back on script.

With any objection, it is important to acknowledge what they said first (so they know you're listening), then pivot to your rebuttal. Let's take a look at the most common objections and how to handle them.

"SEND ME AN EMAIL"

One of the most common objections we hear on the cold call is "Send me an email." This is also the objection reps waste the most time on and often handle absolutely wrong. Usually, when reps hear this, they don't try to fight back, and instead, they listen and send the prospect a canned email or, even worse, spend fifteen minutes writing their own personalized email to the prospect, hoping for a reply. We couldn't think of a bigger waste of time.

If someone says, "Send me an email," ninety-nine times out of one hundred, it means they're not interested and are just too polite to be truthful. Salespeople aren't hired to send emails; they are hired to sell. Unfortunately, reps feel more comfortable drafting up emails than they do cold-calling because they don't have to confront rejection head-on like they do when they speak to someone.

On the cold call, you will handle this objection differently depending on where you are in the script when they object.

In most cases, if you are getting an objection during your intro, your main priority is to advance the conversation to the thirty-second pitch. The prospect needs an idea of what you do to become interested enough to schedule and show up to the demo, and the thirty-second pitch is the best way to convey that information. First, acknowledge their request for an email, then use their request to immediately pivot to your thirty-second pitch.

Example:

Prospect: If you could just send me an email with what your company does, if it is something I am interested in, I will get back with you.

Sales Rep: Sure, no problem. Let me do this. I'll just give you a quick thirty-second description of what we do; that way you can tell me what is most relevant to your needs and what you want more information on in that email. **[THEN JUMP TO THIRTY-SECOND PITCH.]**

After the thirty-second pitch, it is fair game to use CBSs to jump into asking for the demo set. The hope here is something in your thirty-second pitch sparks some interest.

POST-THIRTY-SECOND PITCH

If you have completed your thirty-second pitch and they are still requesting an email, the best thing you can do is emphasize that reading a generic email would take just as long as sitting on a quick product demo, but the email will be much less useful. If they reject the idea, you have a good idea that this prospect was never truly interested in you sending them anything.

Even if the prospect did truly want you to send them something and they were going to review it, you have lost control. They can jump to their own conclusions and decisions based on an email, which won't be enough to sway them.

Example:

Sales Rep: Sure, I can definitely send you something. Anything I send you would still take fifteen to twenty minutes to review, though, and you would likely have a bunch of questions, as it would be very broad and not specific to you. Our product does so many things; you really do have to physically see it in a demo. Let's do this, to be most efficient with your time. When will you be in front of a computer, and when were you planning to read my email? I can just call you then. Does morning or afternoon work better for you?"

Reps must understand that even if they execute a "Send me an email" rebuttal perfectly, it still might only work 10 percent of the time. However, that is ten times better than the less than 1 percent chance the prospect reads their email and decides to email back a day and time that works for them to see a demo. At the end of the day, if all else fails and you have to send them something, the company should standardize what is sent. Reps should only be sending approved templates.

"NOT INTERESTED"

When cold-calling, you will get plenty of prospects who try to cut you off in the beginning and jump the gun on telling you they aren't interested, even when they don't know what you do yet. Don't ever say, "What aren't you interested in? You don't even know what we do." That is a surefire way to irritate them, and the answer is simple: they just aren't interested in anything you could sell them.

To avoid this conflict, we like a direct approach of giving one blunt reason why they might be not interested, followed up with an invitation to expand if that is not the reason. If you get them to talk, it gives you an opportunity to overcome the real objection. That is the key—you just need to buy yourself enough time to find the objection to be able to overcome it. You have to move quickly, or they will hang up. Whatever your rebuttal, your tonality will make all the difference. You want to sound curiously friendly, not disappointed or defensive.

Example:

Prospect: No thanks, we are all set. I am not interested, but thank you. [Notice them using the conversation ender on you this time.]

Sales Rep: Sure, no problem—is that because right now you currently aren't focused on doing more **[NAME SOMETHING THEY MIGHT SPE-CIALIZE IN OR WANT MORE OF]**? What's the situation there?

You want the prospect to say, "No, we can do that, and we are still doing those things. We just aren't interested in [BLANK]." A lot of the time, that [BLANK] will be their contentment with their current tools and processes. They have made up their mind that they aren't interested in changing anything. Which means you will have to get really good at putting people's minds at ease that you aren't asking them to change anything (not on the cold call, anyway) and shift the attention to a thirty-second pitch and why it is in their best interest to just watch a no-obligation free demo.

"HOW MUCH DOES IT COST?"

Want a guaranteed way to get a "not interested" objection on a cold call? Give them pricing after only speaking with them for a minute or two. This is a classic mistake. Do not give pricing to prospects on cold calls. Ninety-nine percent of the time, it does not work out—there is no real context and value to the pricing. That is the reason you have a demo. The demo gives them one hundred reasons to justify the price. The best thing you can do if they ask about pricing during the cold call is deflect and either jump to a thirty-second pitch or go back to emphasizing that they need to see the demo. When you rebut, you want to be vague enough to deflect, then use CBSs to change the subject.

Example:

Prospect: Whatever you're selling, how much does it cost?

Sales Rep: Cost definitely depends on a few factors and what you are currently doing. We cater our plans to customers of all sizes, so don't worry there. Everything we do is extremely affordable, and we can take care of you there; don't worry about that. Let me ask you this: **[ASK A QUESTION ABOUT THEIR BUSINESS TO DEFLECT BACK TO THEM]**.

To deflect, maybe ask them what current tool or software they are using to do X, Y, or Z. Once they answer, get back to the script and either pivot to a thirty-second pitch or set the demo if you have already pitched them. Giving any price will have no value behind it at this point, and they will have no reason to show up for the demo. They will jump to conclusions about whether or not your product justifies that price, and we don't want them to do that. Again, only the demo can justify the price. If they insist on pricing after you've deflected, give them a wide range, starting with your least expensive package and ending with your highest-priced package, and tell them their pricing would depend on many factors that require a second call to determine (setting you up for the demo). If they tell you that even your least expensive package is too much for them, you probably saved yourself some time.

WARM LEADS

As we discussed at the beginning of this chapter, there is a difference in scripting between warm leads and cold leads—specifically the intro. In reality, the intro is the only real difference as far as script structure goes. Of course, warm leads are easier to set appointments with, and the conversation typically flows more smoothly than with cold leads, but that doesn't mean you should change your tactics. You still want to be as professional as possible with them, be as quick and to the point as you can, and not waste their time. The rest of your cold-call pitch (the thirty-second pitch, setting the demo, the wrap-up) should actually be the exact same.

What you don't need for warm leads (especially inbound leads where you're taking a live call from someone interested in your product) are all of the ninja tactics at the beginning of the conversation. You can be more direct about who you are and why you're calling since they inquired about your services. That being said, you should still be quick and to the point. You don't want to waste their time with questions like "How did you hear about us?" or "How are you doing today?" Those questions can take you in nine million different directions and don't keep you in control of the conversation. So, with warm lead introductions, the only difference is that you should acknowledge they inquired about your product and company and then move right into the thirty-second pitch. Here's an example:

Prospect: Hello?

(1) Sales Rep: Hi, Butch?

Prospect: Uh, yes, this is he.

(2) Sales Rep: Hey, Butch, this is A.J. Mahar with Sales Lab Scripting. If you recall, you had inquired about us on [our website/source they came in on]. Does that ring a bell?

Prospect: Oh, yeah. I remember.

(3) Sales Rep: Okay, great. I know you may be busy right now, so why don't we do this? Let me give you a quick thirty-second description of what we do, and if it interests you, we can always set up another time to talk. **[GET INTO PITCH.]**

As you can see, with an intro like this, you're not wasting any time. You acknowledge they inquired about your product or company and where the inquiry came from, helping lower their defenses, then you transition directly into the thirty-second pitch. This allows you to keep control, not get into a back-and-forth conversation, and get directly to what you do.

Too often, we hear warm calls go wrong because the rep starts the call off incorrectly. They usually start by saying some version of "How are you? What made you inquire about us?" and now they're playing the unpredictable fifty-fifty conversation game. They don't know what the person is going to say next, so it's hard to prepare appropriate responses, and from the beginning, they've set the expectation that this is a back-and-forth, fifty-fifty conversation. Which is the exact opposite precedent you want to set. We're the professionals; we're here to control the conversation and accomplish our objective of setting the appointment as effectively and efficiently as possible.

ADDITIONAL RESOURCES

Who would have thought a thirty-second pitch could have so many moving parts? Drafting a script from scratch that incorporates all the insights and best practices we've covered here can take a lot of trial and error. That's why we offer templates and multimedia samples on our website that go far beyond what we have space for here.

> Find examples and downloadable templates of all these techniques at www.Sellfire.com/SalesLabScripting.

For your own scripts, Chapter 5 covers all the best practices to research and fill in the blanks for yourself and your product.

Now that you've seen how your Call 1 script sets up your demo appointment (where your goal is to close the sale), let's consider what that demo should include. We'll cover your Call 2 script in depth in Chapter 3, "Call 2: Running the Demo."

CHAPTER 2 REVIEW

We covered a lot of ground in this chapter, so let's review the key points of an effective cold-call template:

- Call 1 has two goals: setting the demo and getting information to customize the demo. Selling the product is not your goal on this call.
- Call 1 has three (sometimes four) sections:
  - Managing gatekeepers
  - The intro
  - The thirty-second pitch
  - Setting the demo
- Your words and tonality work together to build credibility and put the prospect (or their gatekeeper) at ease.
- Your thirty-second pitch can be longer than thirty seconds, but it should be concise. Don't get bogged down in too much detail.
- Anticipate your prospect's objections before they ever cross the prospect's mind.
- Confidence-building statements (CBSs) are a key means to handle objections.
- Try to make sure everyone involved in the buying decision will be on the demo call.
- Ask for the prospect's personal contact information and a courtesy call to reduce the chances they will no-show the demo appointment.
- Finish the call by building anticipation for the demo and product.

CHAPTER 3

CALL NUMBER 2: RUNNING THE DEMO

In Chapter 2, we walked through the anatomy of Call 1, your cold call to set up your product demonstration. Now it's time for Call 2—the demonstration itself.

Your demo call has two elements:

- A script for your words and tonality
- A visual presentation that gives the prospect a more detailed experience with the product

The demo has one goal: close the sale.

Your script for Call 2 will employ the same principles and techniques as Call 1. The script for Call 2 will be more complex than the script for Call 1, but you will still control the conversation, anticipate objections, and use tonality and psychology to lead your prospect toward a buying decision.

It's helpful to think of your demo call as a video game. In order to win the game (a.k.a. close the sale), you need to earn a certain number of points along the way. Prospect objections are challenges, and if you fail to address them, you lose points. Going off script and missing opportunities to emphasize value lose you points too. The earlier you score points, the greater value they have. You must complete each level to unlock the next one. Earning enough points during the call will lead to a much easier closing. Missing points along the way will leave you with a very lukewarm and apathetic prospect when it's time to close.

If the prospect has an objection or lingering hesitation in the back of their mind, you must address it. You cannot fool yourself into thinking you've moved on and they will forget about it. This is the fastest way of getting the prospect to say, "Thanks for your time. We will review things on our end and get back with you." There are no cheat codes: a rep who skips steps or tries to improvise is most likely going to lose the game.

We believe in logic-based selling. So what is that? Logic-based selling is when your selling points are so perfectly laid out, they seem more like unrealized common sense than selling points. They are almost impossible to ignore because your value propositions are relatable and factual. It is hard to refute a fact.

You aren't simply demonstrating your product. You are demonstrating *why buying your product is in the prospects's best interest*. You ask questions and provide logical answers, and then it's your job to get them to agree with the sensible solution you're presenting. You respond to a prospect's objection with reasons why their concern shouldn't be a concern at all. You demonstrate their return on investment, return on time, or specific ways the product meets the prospect's own stated goals. You explain how the product will deliver on those criteria. If you do it right, not only will the prospect see for themselves that the deal makes sense for them; they will go away feeling like they won.

Building your demo is a big undertaking. It typically takes a month or two to fully flesh out a presentation and comprehensive script. After all, a demo call can take thirty to forty-five-plus minutes, and you need to write every word of it. That's a lot of material, and each section of the script needs to be customized to your product and customer base. First, let's look at the general principles you need to consider when building your demo. Then we'll go over the demo sections one at a time.

SETTING THE STAGE

At the end of Call 1, you sent the prospect a calendar invitation. That invite should contain the video link for your meeting. We recommend the sales rep always be on camera for Call 2 if possible. It gives a human element that helps create a personal connection with the prospect. Some prospects may not be comfortable on camera, and it's important to acknowledge they don't have to be if they don't want to. But it's preferable for them to be on camera as well so you can monitor their facial expressions and body language.

The only time a rep shouldn't be on camera is in the unlikely event they can't present themselves in a professional way for some reason. It's not necessary to wear a suit and tie or look like you're in an office—the mass movement to remote work has changed expectations about appearances. But the rep should be tidy and polished, with a neutral or company-branded background. If your company is casual, a company-branded shirt is a good choice.

TONALITY

When you're running a demo, especially when you're explaining features, you want to sound like a product expert. You do not want to come across as a "typical salesperson," where you're trying to be "buddy-buddy" with the prospect or oversell your product. Remember, you need to think of yourself as an actor auditioning for the role of a supersharp, articulate, and confident industry expert.

Your scope of knowledge and passion for the product need to give the prospect confidence. We often hear prospects say they were hesitant about buying at first, but the rep's overwhelming confidence in the product was the reason they moved forward. In Chapter 2, we discussed how you can project a professional image even when the prospect can't see you. The same concepts hold true for your demo (especially if they *can* see you on video). You should be upbeat and confident and come across like you love your job, the company you work for, and the product. When it comes to spending money on a product, you have to understand the prospect is likely hesitant. Your confidence in and excitement for the product, expressed over the course of the demo, should decrease that hesitancy.

Common mistakes with tonality include projecting a "bro" attitude—too casual, too social, or acting as if the prospect is a personal friend. This isn't the place to ask about their kids or family or try to find common interests in the name of "building rapport." This isn't relational selling, where it takes months or years to close a deal. The prospect will subconsciously know you're only acting that way to make them like you so they'll buy from you at the end of the call. It comes off as disingenuous and hurts you more than it helps. The prospect doesn't need you as a friend. They need your product for their business, so stick to the script.

What if the prospect brings up something off topic? If they ask, "Hey, where are you from?" You should absolutely acknowledge and answer them. But you don't need to make it a long conversation. Address them politely but steer the conversation back to the script and your product as quickly and professionally as you can.

Another common mistake is sounding like a "nervous novice." Speaking too quietly or timidly, stammering, or using lots of filler words like "um" and "uh" destroy your credibility. This often occurs when you don't know your script or pitch very well. If you find yourself stammering through your script, you need to practice more and really understand the words you're saying.

Which brings us to the last important piece of tonality—your energy. We've heard so many sales reps who sound like they're having a bad day or don't like their job. If you lack energy on the phone, you'll lull your prospect to sleep, and they'll tune out. At the same time, you don't want to go overboard either. If you think you sound too enthusiastic or you try to persuade someone with your tone, you've probably gone too far. It comes off as "salesy" and disingenuous, and the prospect can subconsciously feel that, even through the phone. You need to find a healthy balance.

CONTROL THE CONVERSATION

In Call 1, we discussed how you control the prospect's path through the "flowchart" of the call by asking closed-ended questions. In your demo, it is harder to control the conversation, but your aim is still to manage the prospect's attention and the way they process information.

There's a time to talk and a time to shut up. A good script

will show you exactly when to do both. In those moments, you are controlling the prospect's attention and giving them the opportunity to engage with your product mentally and emotionally.

The analogy we like to use is test-driving a car. First, the sales rep drives, and the prospect is the passenger. That's the time to talk and explain all the features—point out the comfortable seats and the quiet engine. Then the rep and the prospect change places so the prospect can drive. That's when the rep needs to be quiet. As the prospect drives, they take mental ownership of the car. They feel the pedals. They imagine themselves driving home from work. The last thing a rep should do is burst that bubble by interrupting or making a bunch of small talk. You'll yank them right out of their imaginary happy place, where they're falling in love with that car.

Controlling the conversation during sales calls works the same way. As you present the product and explain it, you direct the prospect's attention, and it's crucial they go on this mental journey with you. They should be picturing all the ways this product can benefit their business. A solid script limits the questions you ask and targets the prospect at exactly the right times so the prospect doesn't have to change gears to answer questions when they should be falling in love with the product.

Many sales guides encourage a fifty-fifty conversation, where the rep and the prospect contribute equally, to make the prospect feel heard. Our system is closer to eighty-twenty or ninety-ten. The rep checks in from time to time that their pitch is making sense. But if you are addressing the prospect's questions and objections up front, they already feel heard. The rep does most of the talking and guides the conversation where they want it to go.

Think of the script as a story you're trying to tell or presentation you're trying to deliver. A great story can take several minutes or even hours to tell (think of a good movie). Telling a story requires you to almost share a consciousness with the audience—a good storyteller or presenter will have you hanging on the edge of your seat as they paint the exact picture they want you to see and take you on a mental journey with them. Sometimes stories require quick check-ins to make sure the audience is on the same page, but they rarely require a back-and-forth dialogue. That's exactly what you want for your presentations. You have a beginning, middle, and end with very specific points you need to make—you cannot have a fifty-fifty conversation and allow the audience to derail your story. There will be times you'll need to ask a prospect for specific information to inform the presentation, but most of your demo should be you guiding the prospect on the mental journey you need them to go on—the story of how your product will solve their issues, told while you simultaneously anticipate and proactively handle their hidden objections.

Proactive Objection Elimination versus Reactive Objection Elimination

Most sales books provide guidance on how to handle objections at the end of your pitch. However, our philosophy aims to avoid objections in the first place. While it's nearly impossible to eliminate objections entirely, we have developed a powerful strategy called "proactive objection elimination" that significantly reduces the number of objections you get at the end of your pitch. This approach involves anticipating common prospect objections and addressing them proactively by scripting strategic responses to those objections throughout your demo. By doing this, you address the most common objections before your prospects even have a chance to raise them. This, in turn, eliminates most of the objections you'd normally receive at the end of your pitch and makes for a much smoother close.

We also call this the 8 *Mile* approach to selling. In the movie 8 *Mile*, Eminem's character, B-Rabbit, demonstrates a powerful parallel to our approach of proactive objection elimination. If you haven't seen the movie, it's about rappers competing in a freestyle battle competition where each person disses another via freestyle rap, and the crowd decides the winner of each matchup. B-Rabbit beats all his opponents and makes it to the very end of the competition. During the final, climactic battle, he takes a unique approach to disarming his opponent. Instead of doing what everyone else does, a freestyle diss about his opponent, he takes the mic and freestyles a rap that proactively addresses his own flaws and vulnerabilities. By doing so, he removes the ammunition from his opponent's arsenal. This strategic move catches his opponent off guard, leaving him speechless and unable to effectively counter. B-rabbit wins the battle.

Our proactive objection elimination strategy follows a similar principle. By anticipating and addressing common objections before prospects have a chance to raise them, you take control of the conversation and neutralize potential objections. Other benefits of this approach are that it demonstrates credibility and builds rapport with your prospect. When you proactively understand a prospect's objections, you demonstrate that you know their situation, understand their problems, and have solutions to make their lives better. It's the same psychological effect as when you finish someone else's sentence: you get them.

From a tactical standpoint, proactive objection elimination needs to be implemented throughout your Call 2 presentation.

The best way to implement it is through a three-step process. The first step is to identify the objection you want to eliminate. The second step is to eliminate the objection by proactively writing the rebuttal into your script. And the third and most important step is to check that it resonated with the prospect and they agree with your rebuttal.

Here's an example:

Step 1: The objection we want to eliminate is "I don't want to go through the pain of switching software."

Step 2: You dedicate a section of your script and presentation to explaining how a lot of prospects you speak to (just like your prospect) fear switching software because of the issues they dealt with when onboarding previous companies (competitors of yours). After that, you go into why that would not be the case with your company. For example, "I speak with a lot of media companies that tell me the only reason they are with their current software is that they really don't want to go through the hassle of changing software again, even if their current software is not the best one out there. They talk about how difficult their current software was to set up originally, how long it took to get their staff trained on it, and how it sometimes was a nightmare to get their prospects transitioned to it. So here is what we do to make sure our prospects don't have those issues and instead have a world-class experience transitioning to our platform." Then you outline the onboarding experience, show how impressive your timelines are, and provide some social proof—perhaps quotes from current prospects about how hesitant they were to switch but how happy they are that they did.

Step 3: You end the scripting with a question like "Does that make sense?" to make sure the script resonated with the prospect and the objection is, in fact, eliminated. So, sticking with the current example, at the end of your section of the script talking about how great your onboarding is and how prospects are so happy they switched, you finish with the question "Does that make sense?" and wait to hear their response. If you get a convincing or confident "Yes, makes sense," you know you've made your point and you've successfully eliminated the objection.

However, if they say no or give an apathetic "Sure" or "I guess so," you know you have not eliminated that objection. If that happens, you have to address it right there. You can't just move on to the next part of the script. This is where most sales reps fall short. You have to either ask the prospect more questions to understand what didn't make sense or rephrase the statement and check whether that put you on the same page and they now agree with you. Otherwise, the prospect will be distracted, thinking of that objection (and not your product demo) for the rest of the presentation, and it will be much more difficult to close at the end of your presentation.

We often call this process "closing the door." Think of your sales script as navigating a long hallway toward a sale. The hallway represents the journey, and on either side, there are open doors representing potential objections. As you progress through your script, you encounter these potential objections, and your task is to address them effectively, symbolically closing each door. The closing of the door is getting the emphatic yes from your prospect when you ask them, "Does that make sense?" When you reach the end of the hallway, if all the doors are closed, you have successfully handled all the objections and can smoothly secure the sale. However, if you leave a door open, meaning you neglected to successfully address an objection, the prospect may walk through that door and away from you, resulting in a lost sale. The confirmation you receive from your prospect in Step 3 is confirmation the door is closed. Doing this three-step process is a key component to a successful script. Do not skip it.

SIMPLE, EFFECTIVE VISUALS

There's an art to choosing visuals that will connect with your prospects and be persuasive. We find a lot of product demos are much too complicated. Your presentation must allow the prospect to breathe and visualize themselves using the product. If each feature has many different options, it can quickly become overwhelming and leave the prospect feeling confused, defensive, or with too many unanswered questions.

Don't use paragraphs of text the prospect is supposed to read off the screen (they likely won't). Your presentation should focus on images with a few titles while they hear you explain things. The text and visuals in your presentation slides should be clear and match your verbal script. You don't want to be talking about something on the left side of their screen while the prospect is fixated on something to the right.

As mentioned earlier, think of yourself as a storyteller taking the prospect on a journey. You should be controlling the prospect's thought process at all times with the words in the script and the visuals you present. Don't introduce noise or friction by having complicated and busy visuals. Make sure the visuals reinforce exactly what the prospect is hearing and nothing more. If the product is a software solution, it's a good idea to spend some time demonstrating features live in the software, but that should not be your entire presentation. A combination of presentation slides and live demo is a lot more effective.

You also need to ensure your visuals or screenshots are clear and easy to read, even on smaller screens. When you share your screen, images get even smaller, so the layout should be simple and clean. A software screenshot doesn't necessarily need to show the user's whole view. You can zoom in on a particular detail you want to discuss as long as it's easy for the prospect to see what you're talking about.

The slides should be branded to your company's colors and logo but in a tidy, professional way. You don't want things to look slapped together. You need a polished slide deck.

TIMING

As you develop your demo script, you'll need to find the sweet spot of how much information to include and how long the presentation should be. Those will depend on a number of factors, including whether the demo was set from a cold call or inbound inquiry, the complexity of the product, and industry standard expectations for this type of demo.

If your demo is too short, the prospect won't get enough information to make a decision. On the other hand, if you push the prospect's attention beyond the expectations of the industry and show no signs of wrapping up, you risk having them zone out or cut you off. The sweet spot we've found for most demos is between twenty-five and thirty minutes reading straight through, which translates to forty to sixty-plus minutes in real time depending on the number of questions and side conversations you have with the prospect. But those numbers can vary, as we mentioned—just make sure you're factoring questions and objections into your time expectations.

Over time, your company will probably introduce new products and features. You don't want to keep adding more and more slides to your presentation until it becomes unwieldy.

You'll need to continuously curate the demo and replace some older features with new ones so you're always showing a selection of the best your company has to offer.

Our experience suggests you should finish your discussion of features and timelines (Sections 4 and 5) and be ready to discuss pricing (Section 7) about three-quarters of the way through your allotted time. That leaves a margin (Section 6) during which you can answer questions, overcome objections, and get the prospect signed up.

STEP BY STEP

Your demo call will follow the structure of your visual presentation, and it must always contain the following sections:

1. Branded cover page
2. Agenda
3. Credibility
4. Product walk-through and/or live demo
5. Timeline (next steps)
6. Trial closing
7. Pricing
8. Transition to Close

Let's look at the eight sections of your demo in detail.

1. BRANDED COVER PAGE

The first visual you want to show the prospect is a title slide containing your company branding and personalized touches relevant to the person you are pitching. You want to include the prospect's name, company name, and company logo (if it's easily taken from their website) so they can see the presentation was customized for them.

For example, your cover might say "Prepared for A.J. Mahar & Butch Hodson, Sales Lab Scripting" and include our company logo. This slide takes seconds to make, but it adds a lot of professionalism and positive impact to your demo. It reinforces your assertion in Call 1 that you would spend time preparing for this meeting and customizing the demo and separates you from other companies and salespeople who don't go the extra mile.

2. AGENDA

It's important to have an agenda for each presentation because it sets the tone and the prospect's expectations for what you'll cover during this presentation. Having a clear agenda helps the prospect understand you are in the driver's seat and reassures them you are going to use their time effectively.

We've seen many companies run demos without clarifying the agenda up front, and it's usually a mess. When you don't set the stage and tone of the presentation, the prospect almost always takes control of the demo and jumps in to ask questions immediately. This often leads to the prospect bouncing from topic to topic and inevitably asking about pricing and cutting the presentation short. When this happens, there's no way to stay on script. Without any consistency in the presentation, important steps get forgotten, and the chances of closing that sale drop dramatically.

As we mentioned earlier, think of your presentation like a movie: there is a beginning, middle, and end. You're telling a story, and each slide is strategically placed to build upon the next, just like the scenes in a movie. You can't start a movie 75 percent of the way through, then rewind back to the beginning, then fast-forward to the end and have it make sense. The same goes for your demo. You can't bounce around and jump to pricing—skipping to pricing will tank your close rate. You want a professional demo run by a professional salesperson covering the topics you want to cover in the sequence you want them covered. That's what the agenda allows you to do. It sits the prospect down and says, "This is my movie, and here's how you should watch it."

The agenda slide shows there will be three parts to the presentation:

A. Getting to Know You
B. Getting to Know Us
C. Pricing and Next Steps

You will work through the "Getting to Know You" section while the agenda slide is up. The "Getting to Know Us" section, which includes your credibility slide and the product demo, is the main body of your presentation and should take up roughly 80 percent of your presentation. The section on "Next Steps'" will cover your timeline slide, and pricing will follow.

You should quickly introduce the three parts and jump right into the first section. It should sound something like this:

Sales Rep: Okay, so you should now see my screen where it says agenda. I just want to take a minute or two to confirm a few things about you and your company and make sure we are all on the same page. After that, we'll dive into Sales Lab Scripting and our full product suite. That will be the majority of this presentation. At the end, we will go over exactly what you can expect if you decide to partner with us and what those next steps would be.

Couple of questions for you before we get started.

Agenda—"Getting to Know You"

While the agenda slide is still up, you should go straight into the first section of the script. Normally, the sales rep should be talking 90 percent of the time. However, during this part of the presentation, the roles are reversed and the rep needs to gather information from the prospect, so listening to the prospect is important. During this section, you should ask questions or confirm information about the prospect's business you might not have had time to cover on Call 1. The important thing to remember is you're not here to confirm information or ask questions just to ask them. Each question you ask or piece of info you confirm should have a very specific purpose behind it. And that purpose is to close the deal.

So if you ask which software they're currently using, it's because you're going to show them later in the presentation how what you are offering is better than what they are currently using. If you ask what types of jobs they'd like to be doing more of, it's because you're going to show them how your software can help them get those jobs. If you ask what their average order size is and what their normal close rate is when someone calls looking for their services, it's because you're going to show them at the end of the presentation in a return on investment (ROI) calculator that your company will help them get X many calls, which means, with Y close rate, they'll have Z ROI. Every question is deliberate, and there is no fluff.

You'll confirm (if you already got this information on Call 1) what software, platforms, and tools they currently use for their business processes; what problems they're trying to solve; what is most important to them; what their average order size is; and whether they have plans to grow or scale and, if so, what their capacity is to take on new business.

For example, let's say your product caters to media companies and helps them with online ordering, scheduling, invoicing, and payment processing—all of their day-to-day logistics. You would confirm what the prospect is currently using for online ordering and how they are doing scheduling, invoicing, and payment processing. You'd also ask how many team members they have and what platform they use to deliver their content to their prospects—anything you can find out about their current workflow and any hurdles that come along with it.

It's important to remember that how you phrase these questions and how you sound when asking them are critical. You want to come across with genuine curiosity, like a doctor learning more about a patient's symptoms. You want them to see you as someone there to help them come up with a solution to their problems. You don't want to sound like a prosecutor cross-examining them and trying to get the prospect to slip up so you can send them to jail.

Equally important is the amount of time you spend on this section. If you're spending ten minutes randomly asking question after question without any end in sight, the person is going to feel like you're wasting their time. They're going to rush you to get on with the presentation. You want to avoid that at all costs. You should have this part nailed down quickly and efficiently in five minutes or less. Lay the groundwork by prefacing the questions with a time stamp.

> Sales Rep: Okay, great. I have a few very quick questions that will help me determine what to focus on in this presentation and be most effective with your time today.

Then ask your questions. Once you're confident you have all the information you need, you can transition into incentives.

Agenda—"Getting to Know Us"

This section of the script is very brief but lets the prospect know the majority of the presentation will be the sales rep presenting the product and driving the story.

Agenda—"Pricing and Next Steps"

The third and final script section accompanying the agenda slide is where you let the prospect know we're not going to jump around and we'll talk about pricing and next steps at the very end of the presentation. We already talked about why that's important at the beginning of this chapter. Additionally, right before you transition to the next slide, you'll hint that there are incentives (like a discount or an added feature) for the prospect if they love everything they see. We'll talk more about incentives in Chapter 4, but it's important to have a sense of urgency at the end of the presentation for a prospect to buy. Time-based incentives reward the prospect for coming on board sooner rather than later. They also allow prospects to feel like they are winning by making a quicker decision. Once you've finished describing the incentive, it's time to jump into the main body of the demo, where the prospect gets to know you. Here's an example of how the pricing and next steps section should sound:

> Sales Rep: Okay, great, that's all the information I need. I think you're going to be really impressed with what we have. Now let's jump into how we can help.

3. CREDIBILITY

The next slide is typically devoted to building credibility for your company. This can be one or two slides and often includes the names and photos of the CEO and founders along with a brief background of the company's mission and history. Adding photos brings a human touch of "We are real people; these are the faces of the company." The reasoning behind this is no different than when companies put "about us" or "meet our team" pages on their websites. This is also where you can quickly share positive reviews, awards you've won, case studies and outcomes, or data and trends that show your company in the best possible light—especially if you have impressive customer-retention stats. If you have a customer with a national name or if there have been any good quotes about you in the media, the credibility slides are a good place to put them. Including information about well-known customers or a deep base of smaller customers builds social proof that your product works.

These elements demonstrate that your company is well established, reputable, headed by experienced people, and has a base of happy customers. This closes the door on a host of potential objections, especially if the client wasn't already familiar with your brand. Now they can see you are not some fly-by-night operation that's going to take their money and run.

When discussing your happy customers, be sure to talk about them in terms your target customer can relate to. The customer needs to know that people *just like them* use your product and love it.

If you're not well established and you only have a small customer base, there are ways to highlight the benefits in that. You can separate yourself from the big companies by saying you're a smaller team that provides amazing customer service, can cater to changes, and has the ability to innovate quickly.

You can sell how personalized and hands-on your company is with clients. You can pair this with customer quotes for social proof that customers just like them love working with a company like yours.

4. PRODUCT WALK-THROUGH AND/OR LIVE DEMO

After your credibility slides, it's time to show off the product. Remember, the purpose of your demo is not to show off every possible feature of your product—it's to show the prospect why making this purchase is the right decision for them. Some products are so complex or robust it would take hours to walk through every feature. That's just too much information and too much time. Focusing on the most popular and broadly useful features will be plenty.

You can show off your product in a few ways. You can create slides, show a live demo of your product, or do a combination of both. The benefit of showing slides is that you can doctor them to show exactly what you want to show in the exact sequence you want to show them in so you can tell the exact story you want to tell. The negative is that the prospect doesn't get to see and feel what the product looks like in real life.

The benefit of a live product demo is that you can really paint a picture of how the product looks and feels for your prospect. On top of that, if you're showing a live account, the prospect can see the product working in real time for a business like theirs—again, social proof. The downside of a live product demo is it's easy for the prospect's imagination to run wild. They may start asking too many questions and want to jump around to see how the different parts of the product work. If this happens, you can quickly lose control of the conversation. It could potentially be difficult to get back on script. The important thing to remember when doing a live product demo is to strategically show the same features in the same order.

When presenting your product, you should highlight the features that anticipate the objections you think the prospect may make and that you identified in your research. That way, as you go over each feature, you simultaneously bring up questions or concerns and address them before the prospect can bring them up (and sometimes before the prospect thinks of them). This increases their confidence in you and the product and reduces the number of objections you'll need to handle at closing.

Put Your Best Features Forward

You want to lead with your most impactful features first. Consider the game-changing things that make your product stand out from your competitors and drive a great ROI for the customer.

Sometimes sales reps leave the best for last because they want to build momentum before they talk about pricing. We advise the opposite. This is going to be a long call. The prospect has already listened to several minutes about your company and your prospect base. You set up the meeting with an expectation that it would last fifteen or twenty minutes. If you want the prospect to stay with you for the full forty-five minutes to an hour, they need to be fully engaged and interested in what they're hearing. Don't make them wait for the good stuff.

If your product is a piece of software, you might demonstrate those features live in a demo account rather than just talking through the features on slides. The process of logging in to the account can be a valuable "test drive" experience that allows the prospect to imagine themselves using the product. However, once inside the demo account, you should show off the best and most useful features first.

The research you'll do on your prospects and competitors will help you determine your strongest and most distinctive features. Whatever problem your product solves, ask your prospect to describe how they're solving that problem right now. Then show them how your product does it better, faster, and/or easier. And of course, end with a "door closing" question like "Does that make sense?" to make sure they agree your solution is better.

The exception to this rule is if you have a product that requires you to use it step-by-step. In that case, you should logically demonstrate the product from first use all the way to the end, walking them through each step. For example, if you have a software product that performs scheduling, estimates, invoices, and payment collection, you would want to tell the story by demonstrating the product in that order. You can't get to a payment collection without first sending an invoice. You also wouldn't be sending an invoice without first scheduling an appointment with that customer to give them an estimate. Telling the story in the order the product is used allows the prospect to visually understand the product in a more valuable way.

Setting Expectations

In Chapter 1, we discussed the importance of setting correct expectations with the prospect. We recommend against using visuals from a real prospect account for this reason. For example, some software companies like to show their features and benefits by letting prospects tour an existing prospect dashboard and see their results.

The problem with this approach is that sales reps naturally tend to choose outliers—the absolute best-performing accounts—rather than typical performers. That can give the prospect unrealistic expectations and hurt prospect retention in the long term. We recommend using a dedicated demo account to give prospects a tour of the features.

Doubling Down

Every aspect of your product might not represent an improvement over the competition's product, but when you have a big advantage, double down on it. After the prospect has explained their current process and you have shown your solution, take a moment. Ask the prospect if your way would be better than what they're doing now. (Sometimes this is called "trial closing.")

You already know the answer is yes. You need the prospect to say it and internalize it. You aren't trial closing the whole product yet or asking the prospect whether the product as a whole is better than their current solution. You're just focusing on one feature at a time. You shouldn't overdo this technique, but just two or three moments of doubling down during the demo will give you a lot of leverage at closing. Make note of them so you can bring them up later.

Trial closing is a good temperature check to gauge the prospect's enthusiasm throughout the demo. If the prospect responds with a resounding yes, you know they are fully engaged and you are addressing their needs. If they give a non-committal or unenthusiastic response, like "I guess so," or if they disagree and say they don't like something, stop. That's a sign the prospect has an unspoken objection. If you proceed without surfacing and addressing that objection, it will build up in their mind. You'll lose their respect and trust, and it will be much harder to overcome that objection at the end of the call. That's when your prospect says they aren't ready to move forward and need to think about it.

Sometimes you'll hear spontaneous reactions from the prospect when a feature really catches their eye or makes an impression. They might say "That's cool" or "Wow, that's amazing!" You should always double down on those unsolicited responses. Agree with them! Tell them how much your customers love that feature, that it's a game changer. The prospect handed you a CBS on a silver platter. Don't waste it.

Momentum and Priming

As you move through your list of eight to ten features, you should be building momentum and sustaining the prospect's engagement. It's a good idea to check in from time to time and make sure they can see your screen and their connection is good. If you move on to a new slide while their video is lagging behind, they'll get confused and disengaged. They probably won't say anything about it unless you ask. You should make sure you and the prospect are (literally) on the same page.

On the other hand, we recommend against stopping the presentation to do a time check. Some reps feel it's a courtesy to ask the prospect how they're doing on time. They might feel like a courtesy, or a good way to "wake up" a prospect who hasn't spoken in a while, but time checks kill your momentum. They take the prospect's mind completely out of the presentation and make them think about all the reasons they might want to end the call. You open the door for them to leave. That's the last thing you want to do! If the prospect truly had an emergency or a hard stop, they'd say so. As long as you're providing value and the prospect is with you, keep going.

As you build momentum, you should also be building the number of yes answers the prospect gives you with questions like "Does that make sense?" You're psychologically conditioning them. We build demo scripts that have many obvious questions to which the prospect could only respond yes. Getting many of those throughout the hour-long demo is an important step. We want their brain programmed to say yes to the things we are asking them, to get them on our side mentally for when we transition to close. The more times in a row they say yes, the harder it will be for them to turn around and say no when you ask for their business.

5. TIMELINE (NEXT STEPS)

When you finish your presentation of features, it's time to show the prospect how long it will take to get the product set up and when they can expect to start seeing results. The prospect needs to have realistic expectations so they can continue visualizing themselves moving forward with the purchase.

Many sales presentations cover the timeline *after* pricing, but this is the wrong approach. We've found through testing and experience that many unspoken prospect objections come from uncertainty about the timeline of product implementation. The prospect may worry about disrupting their current operations with a sudden change. They may be concerned about whether and how the product will integrate with their existing system. They might wonder if they will get enough support for setup and training. Or they may just sense this will be a huge hassle and not want to think about it because they have too much on their plate. If you leave timeline until after pricing, most prospects aren't going to articulate objections like this because they don't want to be confrontational or sound indecisive. They'll just make vague excuses and get off the call. We've found that making time to clarify your timeline eliminates a lot of prospects' unspoken and often unfounded objections up front, before it's too late.

For this slide, you'll lay out a clear perspective on what will happen over the next thirty, sixty, or ninety days (or however long your setup takes). You'll explain your rollout, onboarding, and training process step-by-step: when they'll be contacted by customer service or the integration team, how long the setup will take, and so forth. You'll also set clear expectations on when they will start to see results and how long it will take to maximize their results. All of this information helps build their mental image of what it will be like to own and use the product.

Explaining the timeline is also a great opportunity to prime the prospect for closing. For example:

Sales Rep: So let's say, hypothetically, here you said, "Okay, Butch, the product is amazing; everything looks great; we are ready to move forward." If that were the case and we got your green light, here is what those next steps would look like.

You're getting the prospect to actively imagine themselves buying the product. You're putting the words in their mouth. You're also reinforcing your name because you want the customer to feel comfortable being on a first-name basis with you by the end of the call. It all contributes to their mental ownership of the product.

6. TRIAL CLOSING

When you finish explaining the timeline, you might stay on that slide for a moment or you might present a slide titled "Questions." Ostensibly, this is the prospect's opportunity to ask any questions you might not have covered. In reality, you're going to ask some pointed questions yourself. This section is your last opportunity to surface and resolve any lingering objections before you talk about pricing. You need to wipe the slate clean of any concerns other than price. You aren't ready to move on until you have a positive signal that the prospect is satisfied with the product and its potential value to their business. Any hesitation or concerns must be addressed before you continue.

Your relationship with the prospect at this point in the demo has evolved significantly since you started. During Call 1 and at the beginning of Call 2, you're in a slightly deferential position. You're asking permission and demonstrating respect for their time. You ask for validation by checking whether things make sense. That's because you haven't provided value to them yet. You haven't sold them on yourself or the product.

Throughout Call 2, you've been establishing yourself as an authority on the product, meeting the prospect's needs, and managing the demonstration process. The more credibility and confidence you build in the prospect, the less deferential and more authoritative you can be. At this point, the prospect should feel like they are in very good hands and that they can relax and process everything they're hearing without having to work to get their questions answered or second-guess your approach. The two of you are collaborating, but you are leading.

You should always be polite and considerate, but you can't be so considerate you back off and let the sale slip away. If you have earned an authoritative position by this point in the call, then you have also earned the right to ask some direct questions and challenge the prospect's thinking—which you will need to do to surface and rebut their objections and close the sale.

Earlier, we described the demo as playing a video game and accumulating points. If you need a hundred points to win and you've done everything correctly up to this point, you might have eighty points by the end of your timeline slide. You need ninety points before you're ready to talk about price. To get those ten points, you need to move through four stages:

- Questions
- Favorites
- Concerns
- Head-to-head comparison

Questions

This first stage gives the prospect a signpost about where you are in the presentation:

> Sales Rep: All right, so we're almost done. We're about to jump into pricing. I know we've covered a lot of information. Do you have any questions for me based on what we've gone over so far?

If they have questions, you'll answer them. Often they don't, but that's not the only thing going on here. This statement signals to the prospect that the presentation is almost over and encourages them to stay engaged with you a little longer. You've been on the call for quite some time, and your prospect may be feeling time pressure. If you jump right into asking them questions, they're likely to say, "Just tell me the price. I'm running out of time." Then the whole conversation is derailed.

This milestone signal is a way of time-stamping the rest of the conversation. It reassures the prospect they won't be on this call all day. It also keeps you leading the meeting and controlling the flow instead of letting the prospect drive the agenda.

Favorites

Now it's time to ramp up. When the prospect has no more questions, you'll ask:

> Sales Rep: So, out of all the things we covered, what was your favorite part?

Psychologically, this question operates on a few levels. First, it asks them to admit there was some aspect of the product that was really cool or appealing to them. They may have been playing those cards close to their chest. Sometimes a reserved prospect will come out of their shell at this point and say they really loved this or that feature. That's great—the prospect is warmer than you thought.

Other prospects may be indifferent and say they don't know. That shows you they aren't in love with the product. You'll have trouble in pricing if they haven't already decided they want it, so it makes sense to pause here. You can be direct with the prospect and tell them that if they don't believe the product is a good fit or will make a big impact for their business, it might not be worth going over pricing at all. Sometimes that's enough to prompt them to say they definitely want to see the pricing. Other times, you might need to turn the tables, call out the disconnect, and ask some more pointed questions to find out what their concerns are.

Concerns

This stage is tricky. It must be delivered in exactly the right words because going off script here can be dangerous.

> Sales Rep: So, based on our product and everything we've gone over so far, is there anything about what we do that you feel would not be a good fit for your business?

If the prospect has any lingering doubts, now is the time for them to speak up. This question is very direct and makes a lot of people uncomfortable. Many reps back off and rephrase the question to make it a softer landing for the prospect. They might ask, "Does everything make sense?" or "Is there anything that doesn't make sense?"

These phrases were appropriate early on in the process, but they're much too vague to be effective here. Many reps think an agreement here is a buying signal, but that's not true. The prospect could agree that everything makes sense, but that doesn't mean the prospect likes the product or believes it is right for them. It just means you were clear in your explanation.

> Sales Rep: Is there anything we do that would not be a good fit for your business?

This is much more specific. If they say no, it means everything you do is a good fit. If they do mention one or two things, that's still a useful answer. Those are objections you can rebut and overcome, and you can't move forward to the next stage until you do. Remember, the golden rule of closing is you cannot go into pricing with a seed of doubt or concern remaining about anything else.

Head-to-Head Comparison

If everything is resolved so far, the final stage is the most direct and involves the hardest question of all. There's no sugarcoating it. Many sales reps struggle to ask this one—some just skip it because they're too uncomfortable. But you can't back off now.

Sales Rep: All right, we're about to jump into pricing, so my last question for you is after everything we've gone over, do you believe our product is a better fit and would be better for your company than what you're currently doing?

If they are using a competing product, you can name-drop it. If they are working with some solution of their own, the phrase "what you're currently doing" will cover it. You're really asking the prospect to lay their cards on the table now and decide whether your product is better than their status quo. If they agree, they're admitting they want the product.

There are different types of answers that could come up here. A lot of prospects will hedge or give a lukewarm response. That's not good enough to proceed. You need to push for a direct answer. For example, a prospect might say some variation of "Yeah, I like what you have, but I'll have to see the price and compare."

Well, that's not what we asked. We didn't ask if you like it or which one is more affordable. We asked which one is the better product or process for them. If you're not getting a very clear answer, like "I like your solution better than what I'm doing right now," you need to double back and get clarification. It might feel uncomfortable, but it's absolutely necessary. A good way to do this is to say something like "Okay, so let's just hypothetically say both solutions didn't cost anything, and you were comparing the two products head-to-head. Which do you think is a better solution for you?"

You wouldn't want to suggest imagining that they cost the

same because they probably don't cost the same, and if your product costs more, you've opened an exit door for the prospect. By imaging they're both free, you create an even playing field. You're trying hard to recruit them onto your team.

If the prospect has any answer other than a definite "Yes, yours is better" by this point, then nothing you presented caught their interest and persuaded them, and you have to go back through your product offering and find out where the disconnect is. If you go into pricing without that yes, you'll wind up hearing "Thanks, I'll think about it."

For more guidance on surfacing and rebutting objections, see Chapter 4 and the resources on our website, www.Sellfire.com/SalesLabScripting.

7. PRICING

Once you have approval from the prospect, you're ready to present your pricing. Well, you're *almost* ready. Once you put prices up on the screen, your prospect is going to fixate on those numbers. They'll immediately start doing mental math on their budget, their current bank balance, and whether they can afford the product. You won't be able to make any other points because they won't hear you. So you have to make sure the prospect understands the product's value before you show them the price.

Return on Investment

In order for someone to buy something, they must believe the value they're getting is greater than the price they're paying. Even when people make wasteful money decisions, they intend to get *something* out of it. A luxury sports car provides an ego boost. Gambling provides a thrill. Nobody wants to just set their money on fire and get nothing in return. Without a good enough ROI, price doesn't matter. The price could be $50 or $500 or $5,000, but if the prospect doesn't perceive value in it, they won't buy.

Whenever you talk about price, you need to put it in the context that this isn't just an expense for the prospect. It's an investment that will bring a return. That return might have a clear financial impact, such as bringing in more revenue or cutting their costs. But what about products that have less of a direct impact on the prospect's bottom line, like saving time or making processes easier and more efficient?

You need to find a way to express that benefit in financial or practical terms. For example, if I have a big yard, it might take me five or six hours to mow the grass. If I mow once a week, that's twenty or thirty hours a month. If I could pay $400 a month to a lawn service instead, I could use those thirty hours to make a lot more than $400.

One way to make this point visually is to use an ROI calculator. It's basically a glorified spreadsheet with the formulas already built in. From your research, you should already know your typical inputs for this prospect, like the type of clients they want to bring in, their average order size, or how much they make per hour. You can use this to show that if the product helps them win more jobs or increase their capacity by X, they will increase their revenue by Y. Then you can compare that result to the price of your typical product package (this also helps anchor the price in the prospect's mind). Your ROI could also be based on the owner's time or their employees' time. The formula would reflect how much their time is worth—not just their normal rate but the opportunity to use that time for something more valuable. If the projected ROI is three to one or four to one (or more), it gives the prospect a very logical reason why the purchase makes sense.

There's an important psychological technique to presenting an ROI calculator. When you ask the prospect to project their success with the product, always come back with a *more* conservative estimate to put into the formula (as long as the numbers will still work in your favor). If your project brings in client leads, you might ask their closing rate. If they say, "Eight out of ten," cut it in half:

> Sales Rep: Okay, well, let's say *even if* it were only four out of ten, that's four new jobs per month.

If your product saves time, you ask how much time they spend on a task. Again, you reset their estimate to a more conservative number. If they say they spend one hundred hours a month on a task, you calculate for *even if* your product only saved them fifty hours a month. It silently invites the prospect to do their own mental math. If your calculator shows that four new jobs a month would produce an ROI of 300 percent on the product, they will mentally rerun that calculation based on their original projection of eight new jobs a month. That's a 600 percent return! If you show that saving fifty hours has an ROI of four to one, they'll tell themselves that it's really one hundred hours and eight to one. But *you* didn't make those huge promises to them. *They* said it to themselves.

This helps build your credibility because you are clearly not trying to overpromise anything. You're not padding your estimates to make the product look better—quite the opposite. You're setting realistic expectations for their customer experience. As discussed in Chapter 1, customers who have unrealistic expectations wind up dissatisfied, even with excellent performance. You must set the right expectations to retain happy customers long-term. Good customer retention is where you make all your money.

Now, you must also consider that some prospects have goals that are more personal and valuable to them than money. If they saved twenty hours a month, maybe they could spend that time with their children or grandchildren. Maybe they could spend more time traveling or check a few experiences off their bucket list. Your product could be bringing them a better quality of life. You'll find out those values early on, when you're asking questions about goals.

There's another interesting aspect to ROI when you're talking to business owners. If you surveyed every business owner in the country and asked if they'd like to grow their business and bring in more clients, you might be surprised by the answers.

A lot of business owners have a mature business that's been growing for a long time. They may have such a great reputation that they're booked out for months or years. They may have reached a stage where they are ready to manage their current book of business and contemplate retirement. They don't want more work. They may not even have the capacity for more work.

But there's a universal ROI that every business owner can appreciate. If you ask any business owner whether they'd like to *do less work and make more money*, there's not one in the whole country who'd tell you no. If you offered them a magic wand that granted them fewer working hours with less stress while making significantly more money than they are right now, every single one of them would say, "Sure!"

No matter what benefit your product offers—whether it's bringing in new prospects, bringing in more high-value prospects, freeing up their time for something more valuable (or enjoyable), or allowing them to upgrade their offerings and charge more for their services—you need to understand the prospect's goals and show how your product gives an ROI that's meaningful to them. Remember all those trap questions we asked during the "Getting to Know You" phase? Now is your opportunity to use that information to show the prospect's ROI for the product.

There are many different ways you could use ROI calculations, either as part of the price presentation or in handling objections to pricing. The best way to use ROI will be tailored to your product and industry, so check out the resources on our website for more information and industry-specific examples.

Package Deals

We recommend offering three packages, each having more features and value than the last: small, medium, and large. You might call them bronze, silver, and gold or silver, gold, and platinum. We don't recommend offering à la carte pricing because you don't want the prospect facing a lot of different choices and decisions at this point. They'll get choice overload and paralysis and lose momentum. Keep them moving down the hallway to the exit and stick to three clear bundles. Don't distract them with too many options.

Position the three in such a way that there's a clear winner in terms of value. The smallest package is much cheaper but only contains the basics. The middle bundle has all the features they need. The most expensive one has all the bells and whistles.

After you go over the product and pricing, recommend the middle package and immediately walk them through the steps to get them signed up. The middle package should always represent the best value. If you recommend the most expensive option, you'll immediately lose credibility. The prospect can see the middle option is the best value, so when your recommendation matches their own opinion, it shows you are both on the same page.

Presenting Each Package

When you reach the pricing slides, don't show all three packages with all the included options and the pricing on the same slide. That's too much information on the screen at once. It would be cluttered and distracting. The prospect wouldn't listen to a word you said because they'd be busy reading all the options.

Each slide should show one package at a time. First, show the description of what's included in the package. You want the prospect's mind focused on your verbal description, not the dollar signs. After you talk it through, then you bring up the price.

There are two different schools of thought on the order in which you should present the three packages. The first way is to present the middle package first—the one you're recommending. Then you show the smallest and describe how it's similar to the recommended package and what's missing. Finally, you show the most expensive package and discuss how it includes everything the middle package does plus some extras. Your recommended package sets the standard, and the other two are described in relation to it.

The second way relies on sticker shock (or "price anchoring"), as recommended by Robert Cialdini in *Influence: The Psychology of Persuasion*.[1] You show the most expensive package first and tell the prospect this package is for large companies that already know about the product and may have used it

---

[1] In *Influence: The Psychology of Persuasion*, Robert Cialdini references studies and foundational psychological research to explain why price anchoring and the principle of contrast are powerful. One notable reference he uses is the work by Amos Tversky and Daniel Kahneman on heuristics and biases, particularly regarding anchoring effects: Amos Tversky and Daniel Kahneman, "Judgment Under Uncertainty: Heuristics and Biases," *Science* 185, no. 4157 (1974): 1124–1131, https://doi.org/10.1126/science.185.4157.1124. This seminal paper outlines how individuals rely on initial information (the anchor) to make subsequent judgments, even when the anchor is arbitrary or irrelevant. Cialdini draws from this to demonstrate how anchoring can influence perceptions of value and pricing in the context of persuasion.

before. Then you recommend the second one, which looks like a much better value by comparison. You might describe that one as being perfect for small to medium-sized businesses. Then you show the third option. It can also be helpful if the middle package is only slightly more expensive than the cheapest one but has many more features. It's the same principle as buckets of popcorn at the movies: you get twice as much popcorn for only 10 percent more.

We've used both methods and recommend you test them in your lab to see which one is more effective for your prospects. Psychologically, the way you present prices can make a big impact. You have the Goldilocks effect: one package is too big and one is too small, so we're programmed to expect the middle one is just right. If you use price anchoring, you can play up the sticker shock even more by setting your prices higher than normal and then offering a discount if they buy today. If your product is membership-based, that could be a lifetime discount, which is even more valuable.

Your prospect always needs a reason to buy today instead of next week or next month. Some other time always sounds more convenient than buying today: in the slow season, they'll have more time to think about it; in the busy season, they'll have more cash flow. If you cold-called them, they don't have a built-in sense of urgency. You can provide that urgency with an incentive structure that makes buying today the most logical choice.

We'll talk more about discounts and incentives in Chapter 4.

Contracts

Some services require the prospect to commit to a contract, and others allow the prospect to opt in month to month. For software sales in particular, contracts really aren't necessary if you have a great product. A month-to-month offer creates a lot of leverage in the pricing phase because it frees up so many options for the sales reps to handle objections.

When the prospect is month to month, you're in a position where you have to keep them happy and ensure they're getting a great ROI. You have to deliver outstanding service every single month to keep them. There are a lot of great talking points here.

It solves many of the prospect's lingering "what if" questions: "What if the product doesn't do what you say it will do?" They can leave.

This ties in to social proof because you can point to your long-term customer base. They wouldn't stay unless your product delivered a strong ROI for them each month. It builds your credibility because you can talk about how it takes three or four months for you to recoup the costs of setting up a new customer—you wouldn't be able to stay in business if your customers weren't happy. It can separate you from the competition because they might lock customers into a contract, but you have to earn their business every month. A month-to-month arrangement puts all the pressure on you and none on the customer, and that gives the customer strong, logical reasons to trust you.

When you're asking prospects to commit to a long-term contract, you lose that negotiating power. You have to rely on a different type of incentive structure, like discounts for prepaying up front or other incentives we'll discuss in Chapter 6.

8. TRANSITION TO CLOSING

After you finish going over all your pricing options, transition to closing. It's important you don't pause or stop after giving the last piece of information about your incentives. If you leave dead air in the conversation, the prospect will think they have to make a decision: yes or no. People hate awkward pauses, and they hate feeling put on the spot. If you leave a gap, the prospect will fill it by saying, "Great, send me a recap of this information so I can think about it."

As soon as the last words about price come out of your mouth, keep talking:

Sales Rep: So here's what I recommend.

As long as you get that sentence out, the prospect knows you aren't done. You can catch your breath. Of course, you're going to recommend the middle package (or whichever package is best for their situation) and recap all the reasons why. You'll point out what a great value it is (especially after the discounts or incentives). You'll emphasize that the features are everything the prospect needs, and you'll double down on one or two items the prospect mentioned that were favorites, game changers, or better for them than their current solution.

Two Paths

There are two main scenarios you might encounter in running a demo. Hopefully, you were able to present to the business owner or head decision maker. Sometimes you aren't able to get the final decision maker on the call, and you're presenting to an office manager, a direct report, or an assistant. We'll call them "non–decision makers." You'll run the presentation pretty much the same way up to this point, but your techniques really diverge in the transition to closing.

Non-Decision Makers

Preparing to close a non-decision maker is a lot more work because you can't *really* close them. You have to persuade them to close the decision maker for you. They're going to have to take all the information from your presentation and pitch it on your behalf to the decision maker. So after you make your recommendation and double down on all the reasons why the product is right for them, there are a couple of specific questions to ask. The first one puts the non-decision maker into the driver's seat:

> Sales Rep: So, [non-decision maker name], based on everything you've seen today, if the owner left this decision completely up to you—I know you don't have the final say, but if you did—would you, personally, move forward with this today?

That's a trial closing very similar to the trial closings we did before pricing. You're taking the person's temperature to see where you stand. They've already said they think this product is better than what they're doing now. What they haven't said yet is that they would sign up if it were their decision.

Just like with the previous trial closings, if there's any hesitation, you cannot move forward. "Probably" or "I'll need to crunch some numbers" aren't good enough. You need a 100 percent "Yes, no doubt." This is a very common mistake we see reps make, and it's a big one. Blowing past a weak response in the trial closing is such a hard habit to break, but it's absolutely crucial to stop and deal with it in the moment. Otherwise, when you get off the call and a few days go by, that "probably" turns into a "maybe," and the "maybe" turns into "maybe not." You can't build a business on "maybe" and "maybe not."

You'll need to surface those unspoken objections in this call—it will be hard to get them back on an additional call. You've been very professional and kept it as quick as possible. You've been transparent and tried to keep them educated and informed. By this point, you've earned the right to be extremely direct in your questions:

> Sales Rep: Feel free to be direct with me, please. What kind of things would influence your decision?

You need to push for answers because if you slack off or get timid at this point, the sale could drag out over months of follow-up calls and back-and-forth conversations. That's not a good use of your time. You might as well know where you stand on this call because otherwise, you'll think you have a deal when you don't.

Once you have the non–decision maker's decision and they've said they would choose your product, the two of you are on the same side. You're a team. They are now going to become your advocate, and you'll rely on them to sell the product in your place.

You can't just send them off to do that blindly. You need to mentally prepare them to present the product to the decision maker, whether that's at a staff meeting, a one-on-one, or wherever they normally give an update on the items that need the decision maker's attention. You must be strategic about this because the first thing your non–decision maker will face is someone saying they don't want to do it! You're preparing them to go into battle.

Sales Rep: So, [name], when you meet with the owner and you tell them you personally love this product, you believe it's a better fit and a great ROI, and you personally recommend they sign up, is there any reason why they would go against your recommendation?

Let's pause to unpack that. You're not saying "if" but "when." You're creating a picture in their mind where they have fully taken ownership of this decision. They can visualize themselves talking to the owner and advocating for the product. You're also coaching them on what to say, in essence giving them a mini sales script.

Then you put them in a slightly awkward position: "Is there any reason they'd go against your recommendation?" They have to stop and think.

Maybe they're in a situation where the decision maker relies on them so much they call a lot of the shots around the office. They might be supremely confident that the decision maker would never go against their recommendation. That's great—it gives us all kinds of flexibility to move forward, and we know we have a good chance at getting a deal.

More likely, they'll start to see it from the decision maker's perspective and tell you the kind of objections the decision maker might have. We call this step "building the plan" because you're walking the non–decision maker step-by-step through their approach to the decision maker.

Perhaps the decision maker won't like the price because they're the one paying. That's your opportunity to give them more ammunition to overcome that objection. Remember, your non–decision maker teammate has only seen the presentation once. They haven't been trained on a full sales script, and they're going to forget things. They aren't product experts, and they aren't going to have a forty-minute PowerPoint presentation to make their pitch—they'll be lucky to get two minutes before they get cut off. You need to pay close attention to the objections they bring up at this point and help them get ahead of those objections with very specific words and ideas for their pitch.

You can also send the decision maker the recording of you presenting your product to the non-decision maker at their company.

For example, if the decision maker thinks the product is too expensive, you can advise the non-decision maker to talk about how frustrating their current solution is and how much time it takes or how it would be a game changer for their clients and bring in a lot more revenue. If your product would free up the non-decision maker's time and energy, they can bring up all the other improvements they could make in the business if they had this product.

Once you've built your plan with the non-decision maker, you need some kind of confirmation they feel good about the plan and their ability to deliver it:

Sales Rep: So do you feel confident now, based on everything we talked about, that if [decision maker] brings up costs, you could show how it's worth it for him?

If they don't, back you go again to solve objections. If they do, you can move on to the next steps. You know you won't be getting a credit card on this call, but you still need to walk the non-decision maker through what needs to happen going forward.

You could reiterate the time frame within which they need to commit to get the discount. You could help them plan what day and time they're going to speak with the decision maker. You could offer to jump on a call with both the non-decision maker and the decision maker at the discussed time. Nine times out of ten, they'll say it's not necessary, but making the offer reinforces that you two are a team and they have your support. If they say "Yes, great!" you can close the decision maker directly.

Decision Makers

If the person you're speaking to has sole authority to make the purchase, you don't need to build a plan. You need to make your own recommendation, recap the pain points (i.e., the problem they are trying to solve and why they are on the call in the first place), and/or double down on the positive things they mentioned during the call. You need to be confident and assume the sale. This is what inexperienced sales reps screw up all the time. They ask generic and insecure questions like "Okay, so what do you think? How does everything look to you?" or "So what are your thoughts?" And 99 percent of the time, the prospect says, "Things look good. I just need a few days, and I'll get back to you."

Instead, you need to lead the prospect through the process of finalizing the sale without any kind of awkward pause or question. For example, you could say something like:

> Sales Rep: Okay, great, to get you started, all I would do here is collect your first month's payment of X amount, and what that's going to do is get you started in our system, and then your account manager is going to call you in two business days to introduce themselves. Is there a good time for them to contact you?

Or you could have them pull up their email to view the invoice. With products at a higher price point, that might involve terms of service or an agreement they have to sign electronically. If it's a lower price point, it might just be a matter of taking a credit card:

> Sales Rep: So, with your green light, I'm going to secure that discounted rate. All we have to do on our end is collect your first month's payment, which will kick-start your account. I'm sending an invoice to your email for the amount of **[FIRST MONTH PAYMENT]**. Which email should I send that to, the **[EMAIL YOU HAVE ON FILE]**?

You prompt them to take action and start the purchase process, and you should not let the person off the phone until you are as far through the payment process as possible. Talk them through every step.

Prospects who aren't really ready to buy will try to end the call early. They'll say, "Just send it to me, and I'll finish it later." They won't. That's an excuse. Politely insist you do it together so you can answer any questions. If the prospect has any objections, you need to bring them to the surface—at this point, you need to force them to either buy or object. Then you can move into objection-handling mode.

THE CLOSING STRETCH

If you've built a good script and tested it thoroughly, by this point in the call, you should already have eliminated or addressed nearly all your prospect's objections. Nevertheless, it's normal to encounter prospects who still resist making the purchase for all kinds of reasons. There are many different techniques and tactics you can use to handle these last-minute objections, and each one should be tested and scripted so your average sales rep can use them successfully. We'll look at the strongest and most effective methods in Chapter 4, "Closing the Sale."

CLOSING THE SALE

When do you close a sale?

Most people believe closing starts at the end of a call. But that's not right. You start closing the sale with the first words out of your mouth on Call 1. Throughout your cold call and demo, all the techniques you use to proactively eliminate objections, control the conversation, influence your prospect's mindset, and address hesitation will pay off at the end of your call in the closing phase. If you don't do those things right, closing a sale will be ten times harder. In fact, with most unsuccessful demo calls we listen to, the sales rep lost the sale long before they even got to the pricing section of the presentation. That's because they didn't get the basics right.

In Chapter 3, we showed how the process of offering discounts and taking payment would work in an idealized scenario where the prospect had few or no objections. In the real world, nine times out of ten, the rep will still have to do some objection handling at the end of the demo. Yes, even with a well-executed Call 1 and a perfect demo, the rep still has work to do at the end. Just being a good "presenter" isn't good enough to reach sales stardom. Sales reps have to be able to turn noes into yeses and "I want to think about things and get back with you" into a "Okay, let's do it." This stage is typically the most stressful part for sales reps, and it is why many people ultimately come to the conclusion that sales isn't for them.

There are so many different reasons a prospect might hesitate or resist buying, so many objections they might raise, that a sales rep must be prepared to move in any direction. A strong sales script will include the right words for overcoming many different objections, but reps still need training and good coaching to be able to choose the right responses.

Each industry, type of product, and prospect base will have certain objections that come up frequently and certain techniques that are most effective. You'll draw on your research and sales lab testing to determine what options your script should contain. That being said, in this chapter, we will simplify things for the rep to uncover the real objection. Then we will implement some strategies to guide the prospect to saying yes while feeling like they won. Here's what we'll cover:

- Uncovering objections the prospect won't tell you
- Aligning yourself as the prospect's ally
- Challenging the prospect's thinking and breaking negative patterns
- Professionally challenging false beliefs
- Creating urgency to close quickly
- Getting managers involved to leverage discounts and build up your product's value
- Why every prospect should get special treatment

THE FAKE OBJECTION

When you face a prospect who's hesitant at closing, you have to realize the first excuse they give probably isn't the truth (or not the whole truth). Most people don't like confrontation, and if they aren't already sold on the product, they don't want to get into a lot of back-and-forth with the sales rep. They just want to keep it brief and get off the hook.

They give vague answers, like "I need a few days to think about it" or "Sounds good. I just need to speak to my partner. Call me back in a week" because it's easier and avoids the discomfort of saying, "I don't think this product will work for me." The problem is those vague answers can trick reps into thinking the prospect is warmer than they actually are and that they still have a chance at closing the sale at a later time. In reality, it's a fake objection.

When prospects give you a fake objection, it doesn't give you anywhere to go. You can't just offer to lower the price. If you offer a discount here, the prospect will have the same response, and you could lose credibility. The prospect will wonder why you didn't give them the best price in the first place. It's not going to make them more interested or increase their urgency.

Instead, what you have to do is uncover the real issue.

THE REAL REASON PROSPECTS WON'T BUY

Behind every single objection you get at the end of your call, there is only one real reason the prospect won't buy from you. And that reason is they're just not 100 percent sure your product or service is going to work for them and give them positive ROI (time, money, value).

How do we know that? Because there's no actual objection a prospect can say at the end of the call that doesn't boil down to that one factor. If someone says, "I just need to think about," would they have to think about it if they knew the product would work for them and they'd get the highest possible return on their investment? No, there'd be nothing else to think about. They'd make more money than they spent, so they'd go find the money to pay for your product or service and net a profit.

Let's look at some other common objections:

"It's too expensive" or "I just don't have it in the budget right now." Would the prospect say that if they knew they'd get a 5x return on their investment? No, because the return they'd get would be 5x more expensive in their favor, and they'd have even more money to spend. So, yes, if they knew your product would work for them, they'd find the money to pay for it. And if they actually didn't have the money for your product, that probably should have been sniffed out before the end of your demo—either while prospecting or on Call 1.

"I just want to do research." Would they have to do research if they knew for a fact they'd get a 5x return? No, there'd be no more research to do. They'd know it would work, and they'd know they'd make money, so there'd be no more research to do, and they'd find the money and pay for your service.

We can go on and on with examples and come to the same result. But how do we get the prospect to tell us the real objection?

There are some false objections that require something we call "isolating the objection."

ISOLATE THE OBJECTION

Let's use "This sounds great. I just need to speak to my partner," as the false objection. When someone says that, we need to isolate the partner's opinion about the product from the consumer's opinion about the product. The way to do that is by giving them a hypothetical situation that sounds like this:

Prospect: This sounds great. I just need to speak to my partner about it.

Sales Rep: Okay, no problem. So before you do that, let me just ask you: let's just say your business partner was on this call right now and said they wanted to move forward with it, and now the decision is only up to you. Would you personally move forward with it, if it were solely your decision?

When you phrase it like that, you've validated what they said about the partner, but you're isolating the objection and getting to the root of the problem—do *they* think it will work and would *they* move forward? If you get an unequivocal yes, they would move forward, then they might actually need to check in with their partner. If they hesitate or say anything else besides a convincing "Yes, I'd 100 percent do it," they're most likely blowing smoke, and you need to uncover the real reason they're objecting.

The partner objection should have been proactively eliminated on Call 1 by trying to make sure all decision makers are on the demo call. Obviously, that cannot happen in all cases, but if it's avoidable, it will eliminate having to deal with this objection at the end.

Now, what if they say something that can't be isolated, like "I just need to think about it"? What do you do then? Unfortunately, it rarely works to come right out and ask, "What is it exactly that you need to think about?" Sales reps say this all the time, but it's an amateur response. That's too samurai. Instead, we need to be ninjas. And the first step to doing that is staying on their side.

STAYING ON THE SAME SIDE

> Prospect: Sounds great. I just need to think about a few things, and I'll get back to you once I look everything over.

You've spent the entire thirty-plus-minute demo on their side. You can't just all of a sudden switch teams and say, "What is it you need to think about?" It sounds defensive and changes the entire energy of the call, and you lose credibility points and the momentum you've been building throughout the presentation. If you respond this way, they will just give you another generic, broad excuse of looking everything over, which won't help you. If you try to push and ask what needs to happen to get a deal done, their radar will go off—you will have turned yourself into a samurai who is coming right at them. And you will end up with the same response: "I told you; I need time to think things over."

In medieval times, if your army was trying to storm an enemy's castle, wouldn't it be a lot easier if their walls weren't up and they invited you in? As a sales rep, you always want to position yourself in a collaborative position with the prospect. You want them to feel that you are on the same team, working together to solve problems. So when a prospect shows hesitation or resistance, respond with empathy. Make them feel heard, and agree that you can see their point of view. Then you can challenge them.

The last thing you want to do is get defensive because you'll wind up in a tug-of-war. Once you validate the prospect's position, you can take back control of the conversation by reemphasizing one of your logical reasons for them to buy today. Here's an example:

Prospect: Sounds great. I just need to go over a few things, and I'll get back to you in a few days.

Sales Rep: Sure, [name], no problem at all. I completely understand. I know this is a big decision you're taking very seriously. We encourage every person we work with to ultimately do what is best for their business and their customers. Let me ask you this. If I were you, this is something I'd have to think through and make sure I felt really good about as well. But one thing I want to ask...

With this statement, you've validated and normalized the prospect's position, which allows you to take back control of the conversation instead of engaging in an adversarial tug-of-war. When you say, "Every person we work with," it foreshadows that initial concerns never prevented others from coming on board. The words "work with" demonstrate the success you have had with other customers. You also stated that decisions should be made based on what is best for the business and their customers.

GET THEM TO TALK

Once you've made the prospect feel comfortable by staying on their side, you can now ask them a lighthearted question that gets them to talk about what their real issue is.

Sales Rep: But one thing I want to ask is when you look at everything we went over today, what do you think would be the one hesitation you have about moving forward with us? Would you say your main hesitation is more of an initial cost concern or a product uncertainty, and you're just not 100 percent sure the product will deliver everything you need? And by the way, it's perfectly okay to be as direct and transparent with me as you want.

At this point, the prospect is going to be a lot more open to giving you clues as to what's holding them back. Sometimes they bring up doors in the demo you may not have closed in the presentation. Other times, they bring something completely different up that was never discussed in the presentation. Either way, you have to address their concern and challenge whatever belief is holding them back. Giving them two options makes it easier for them to pick one of the two or tell you the real reason if it is something different.

CHALLENGING THE PROSPECT

For a sales rep to be good at closing, they have to be comfortable with uncomfortable conversations. That sometimes involves having to disagree with a prospect and convince them to think differently. A good sales rep is defined not just by their ability to turn a no into a yes but also by how they make that shift. They need to challenge the prospect's thinking and help them see things from an entirely different point of view. According to a survey of thousands of business owners described in *The Challenger Sale* by Matthew Dixon and Brent Adamson, prospects actually appreciate it when a sales rep can give them a new perspective on their business and their need for a new solution.[2]

In our discussion of trial closing, we noted your relationship with the prospect evolves over the course of Call 2. By anticipating objections, leading the conversation, demonstrating

---

[2]   *The Challenger Sale* by Matthew Dixon and Brent Adamson is an excellent resource, and the statement aligns with one of its core premises about the value of challenging customer assumptions. Here's how you could reference it: Matthew Dixon and Brent Adamson, The *Challenger Sale: Taking Control of the Customer Conversation* (Portfolio Penguin, 2011). If you're looking for a specific page or section, this idea is introduced in the discussion of the "Challenger Rep" profile, particularly in the chapters about "Teaching for Differentiation" and "Reframing the Customer's Thinking." Depending on the edition, this concept is often highlighted in Chapters 4 and 5.

expertise, and responding to the prospect's concerns, you build up a very high level of credibility. You can be more and more direct, and by the time you reach the closing stage, you can afford to be pretty assertive. In fact, you can't afford *not* to be assertive at this point.

Most reps have good people skills. And the kind of person who cultivates their people skills doesn't enjoy confrontation. They want to be considerate to the prospect. They don't want to put them on the spot or make anyone feel pressured. But being overly considerate in closing will cause sales to evaporate in front of your eyes. It will allow the prospect to put things off, drag their feet, and eventually talk themselves out of the sale. A few prospects will get irritated and leave when a rep is professionally assertive in closing. However, those prospects were likely not going to buy anyway. Even the few sales you might lose are nothing compared to the new sales you gain by challenging the prospect's thought process. Sales reps lose ten times more sales by being too empathetic and passive in closing than they would by being a little too challenging and assertive.

We've listened to so many calls where a sales rep backed down from a prospect's resistance and lost them forever. For example, a prospect might tell the rep they really like everything they see—they are sold on it—but they will have to do a few things first before making the transition, and they will likely be ready to move forward in a month or two. So, as a rep, what do you do? Agree with them that this isn't a priority and they can take all the time they need? If you do, you won't make significant money in sales.

It's vital for reps to understand how to challenge the prospect's thinking, push for real answers, and even interrupt the prospect if need be. And do it all in a polite, professional way.

Sometimes you need to nudge the prospect to open up

about what they're really thinking. Other times, you need to stop them from going into a negative spiral. A prospect who goes on too long talking about an objection will talk themselves right out of a deal that was working for them just fine. There is a fine line, though. If someone is venting about a previous bad experience they had with a competitor, you want to hear them out and let them finish so you know exactly what to address, overcome, and separate. However, if they are going off on a rant you disagree with and spiraling into a negative mindset that isn't correct, you need to interrupt them in a professional manner and stop them before they talk themselves out of the sale entirely. A good professional transition to interrupt someone nicely would look something like this:

> Sales Rep: Hey, I'm so sorry to interrupt you here, but just one thing. I know you said the price is a lot more than your current solution, and it might be a little tough for you. But think about this for just a second...

From there, transition back to the value propositions you need to double down on. Now you're controlling the narrative again, turning it back in a positive direction. An interruption like this is built to be effective and assertive but also polite and collaborative. You excuse yourself. You get permission and time-stamp that you have *just one thing* to add. You validate the prospect's feelings. You don't tell them they're wrong, but you ask them to think about a different perspective. You problem-solve for them. A lot of us are trained that it's very rude to interrupt, but as you can see, there's no rudeness at all. If a prospect thinks you are being salesy or rude, you are doing something wrong.

Challenging the prospect isn't about confronting them. It's about leading them. Once you've changed their direction back to a positive mindset, you can give them more reassurance and CBSs to keep them moving forward. All you're really asking is that the prospect gives you a chance to prove you can deliver on your promises. It's okay to lean on them a bit to get your foot in the door.

There's a fine line between challenging the prospect and pushing them so hard they get upset. If a prospect tells you they aren't going to buy today no matter what and they're going to take time to research and think about it, you need to be judicious in the way you respond. On one hand, you don't want to just lie down and accept it. We have closed many prospects who told us there is no way they would ever buy on the first call. On the other hand, you don't want to be so off-putting they don't want anything to do with you. Whatever objections they give, make at least two or three strong attempts to overcome them with common sense, logic, and the value propositions or pain points we discussed earlier. If that doesn't work, you need to oblige their request and move on to the next prospect because the opportunity presented by the current call is over. You won't close everyone every time, and they won't all be one-call closes. However, there are learnings and findings in every nonsale. Great managers and reps constantly go back to the tape to figure out what they could have done better in that situation.

Missed Opportunity Cost—the Invisible Revenue

One of the most important places to challenge and reframe your prospect's thinking is around their perception of value. You need to replace their concern about *spending* money not just with a hope of gaining money but with a fear of *losing* money—the money they would have gained if they had used your product. Think about it. Most people don't consider themselves as losing something they never had in the first place. We need to challenge that thought process. You want the prospect to believe that if they do something that brings a benefit to them (your product), then by not doing it, they lose that benefit every month (the ROI you would have brought them). By losing that benefit continuously, there is an opportunity cost to not doing something.

We call that potential ROI income "invisible revenue." Prospects naturally have the mindset that they want to save money, so they don't want to purchase an expensive product. But they need to understand that they aren't saving money. They're losing money—money the product would have brought in.

For example, let's say you work for a company that provides leads for real estate agents. The agent you're speaking with told you at the beginning of the call they really want to start getting new business in this up-and-coming part of town where the average commission is around $10,000 a home. If at the end of the call the agent says your product, which is $1,000 per month is just too expensive for them, you can hit them with the invisible revenue scenario:

Prospect: I wasn't expecting this to be $1,000 a month. That's something I'm going to need to think about.

Sales Rep: Sure, I totally understand where you're coming from. It's a big decision for your business. So yes, if you decide not to move forward with us today, you could save $1,000 a month. But one thing to keep in mind is that it also means you're not getting new business in **[INSERT HOT MARKET]** like you said you wanted. And earlier you mentioned that even if you got one new customer in that area per month, you'd make around $10,000 in commission. So, technically, yes, by not signing up with us today, you're not spending $1,000 a month. But think about this: every month someone buys in that area and chooses a different real estate agent who would have chosen you, you are losing out on a minimum of $10,000. So I'd be a lot more concerned with the $10,000 you are losing every month in that area than I would be with just the $1,000. How many customers would you need to buy from you to pay for our service for the entire year? One? The hardest part is just getting your foot in the door in that area; once you do, whatever our costs are, which you could make up immediately...

Let's look at another example. Your product offers online booking for your prospect's website. If their prospect visits the site and the current system is confusing or frustrating (or nonexistent), your prospect's prospect isn't going to pick up the phone and call. They're just going to bounce and book someone else. Your prospect might never even know they were there, but that's a lost opportunity they will never get back. It's the sales rep's job to make the invisible revenue visible by framing the product's value as potential revenue the prospect *should* have but that they're *losing out on.*

Any pain point or goal the prospect expresses can help them visualize invisible revenue. If they mention business is slow and they want more work, you can get them wondering *why* it's slow. Are they doing things (or not doing things) that are blocking the jobs they should be getting? By making invisible revenue visible, you build the case that your product would deliver a lot of value for them. The more value you build in the prospect's mind, the more leverage you have to close the deal.

You can use the same concept with time. If your product can save them time, you can use that "saved time" concept against them. With more time, that prospect can do more of the things they want to do—whether that's making more money, doing different jobs that are more lucrative for them, or spending more time with their kids. By asking the right questions up front in Call 1 and/or your agenda of Call 2, you can position this information in your rebuttals at the end of your presentation.

CREDIBILITY REMINDER

When you're handling objections and challenging a prospect's beliefs at the end of your call, you can't just continue going back and forth with them on the exact same points. At some point, you have to transition and shift their mindset onto something more positive. The best way to do that is to transition into credibility and remind the prospect of the things you talked about during your credibility slide. Or bring up other types of credibility you left off of the credibility slide specifically to use for this part of the call. Once you've made a good and logical point (like the invisible revenue example), you can then follow it up with something like:

> Sales Rep: And like I mentioned earlier, that's why we have over two thousand real estate agents who are paying us on a month-to-month basis. It's not because they're locked into a contract and have to; it's because they are doing the math every single month and seeing that they're making more money than they're spending. So these agents are happy to be paying us, which is also why we have such great reviews like we saw...

Another great credibility reminder is the ROI calculator. Sometimes we won't use the ROI calculator during pricing. Instead, we wait to use it specifically for objection handling. Being able to physically show ROI in an ROI calculator is an extremely successful tool to help close a deal. By padding your rebuttal with social proof or ROI, you're distracting them from their original objection and making the prospect think, "Yeah, if it works for other agents, it should also probably work for me. I don't want to be the dope that gets left behind," helping them get into a more positive mindset.

CREATING URGENCY

Once you've uncovered and handled the prospect's real objections and put their mindset onto something more positive, like a credibility reminder, you shouldn't stop your momentum there and just ask for their business. You need to redirect the prospect's attention again by giving them a logical reason to buy today. In our section on pricing, we discussed the need to incentivize the prospect to purchase immediately or in the very near future (within the week is best). Prospects can always come up with a million reasons why it's the wrong time to buy. We must give them a reason to buy *now*. For products with a short sales cycle, deals that drag out for weeks or months rarely wind up closing at all. And at some point, the amount of time you're spending chasing old business will cost you more than just letting it go and pursuing new business. It just isn't worth pursuing anymore.

So, to minimize purchase hesitation as much as possible, you can easily create an incentive by marking up the base prices on all of your product packages and offering a discount for closing within a deadline. Even if the prospect's original smoke-screen objection had nothing to do with price, it's useful to bring up the possibility of negotiating a discount. It can distract the prospect from their negative thought patterns and give them a sense of anticipation. We often call this tactic "discount as a distraction." Everyone likes the idea of getting a deal. So if you've made some great logical points that make sense for the prospect's objection and then change the subject to giving them a discount, they'll often forget about the objection entirely and start thinking about getting a discount instead. You must overcome the objection first. If you don't and just jump to a discount, they will say thanks but revert back to the objection.

There is another level of complexity here. When a prospect objects, you rebut to overcome. But at the end of the rebuttal, if you just leave it there, it could lead to further debate. We don't want a debate—we want to make our strong point, then change the subject. So the key here is when they object, overcome their objection by making a strong statement then get their mind off the subject by changing the focus to them getting an even better deal. If a prospect decides to stick around and hear about discounts, you know that prospect is closable. And a deal that closes at a slightly lower price than originally anticipated is better than not getting a deal because you were too prideful or stubborn to offer a discount. Sales reps often make the mistake of not discounting because "price wasn't the issue." That is not the only reason we discount.

There are several different ways to present this incentive structure. For higher price points, like software sales, the prospect might need more time to consider overhauling their whole system. You want to make it known that your company incentivizes businesses to come on board sooner rather than later. Typically, you'd offer a five- to seven-day incentive deadline. For subscription service products at a lower price point, you push for a same-day commitment. There are many ways to be creative with this so the prospect doesn't feel it is a pressured, salesy deadline.

However, you want to be very strategic about when and how to use this leverage. The techniques and rebuttals you develop for your script are critical, and you don't want to use all your talking points at once. If your first salvo fails, you have to have others. You always want to have at least one more tactic you can use. Negotiating a discount for the prospect is the last resort.

VISUALS

Your incentives should *not* be shown on your visual presentation. It's a pretty common practice, and designers and trainers often think it's helpful for the prospect to see the higher price struck out and replaced with the discounted price or to have the discounts listed at the side. There are certainly cool things you can do with the graphics. If you go that route, you still want to have pricing you verbally can give them that they cannot see. But we've found it's much more effective to show only one price option on the slide and present your discount verbally.

Think about it. If the prospect can see the discount in the presentation, subconsciously, they realize you must offer the same discount to everyone. After all, it's programmed into the slides. They aren't getting anything special. That can really knock the wind out of your incentive. It's much more powerful for the prospect to feel like they are getting some inside scoop that isn't available to just anyone.

There are so many psychological techniques for managing your prospect's perceptions that there are whole books devoted to the subject. And there are just as many ways to layer them into your scripts. You can find even more detailed script breakdowns in the "Resource" section of our website, www.Sellfire.com/SalesLabScripting.

MAKE IT SPECIAL

One of the most universal psychological triggers is the need to feel special. Everyone wants to be an insider, get an exclusive, have things customized for them. They don't just want a discount—they want a discount other people don't get.

So you don't just offer a lifetime discount out of the blue. You offer a story about why you're going to ask your manager to approve a discount. You want the prospect to feel like you're advocating for them to get special treatment. Then they'll root for you to convince the manager to make a one-time exception.

That's when you can really recruit the prospect to your side. In order for you to persuade your manager to offer this special exception, you and the prospect have to come up with a justification together. You'll go through all the reasons your manager should offer an incentive: how the prospect is a perfect fit for your product, how it would be so impactful in all the ways they shared with you and solve so many problems in their business. Of course, what you're really doing is painting a vivid picture in the prospect's mind of all the value propositions and CBSs they've encountered during the demo. You explain that you'll tell your manager how sure you are that the prospect will love the product even more once they are using it.

> Manager verification of discounts isn't necessarily just a "story." It's always a good idea to make sure reps aren't handing out discounts too quickly. That would be a sign they are failing to build value in prospects' minds. Management might decide to give very consistent reps more discretion in offering discounts without much oversight, but we encourage reps to check in with their manager frequently.

There's another important element to your story: what's in it for you? Obviously, you benefit if the prospect buys. But what makes it worth your while to give the prospect a discount? You need to justify why it would make sense for your manager to approve this special exception. No one will believe you are going to sell something you would lose money on, so you want to add something that will make sense to them. That's usually going to be a story about the prospect's satisfaction and long-term relationship:

> Sales Rep: And then I will tell my manager, after I explain how you are the perfect fit, I will let him know that the hardest part of this whole thing is just getting your foot in the door. Once you are using our software, you will be blown away with the results, and I will make sure to tell my manager that as soon as we do that and you are seeing great results, then you will be a big advocate for us and will do even more business with us in the future. Am I right?

Who would disagree with that? If you crush it for them, of course they'll spend more money with you. It's natural to agree. At the same time, you're putting the image in their head that you *could* really crush it for them. Then you ask the prospect if they can help you win this argument by making a commitment, though we prefer the term "green light":

> Sales Rep: Now, once I do that, and the thing is, if I ask my manager to override some things on the back end and get you this specialty pricing discount, the first thing they'll ask is whether you're going to give us the green light and move forward with us today. So what should I tell my manager if they ask me that?

You need that green light because the last thing you want is for the prospect to hear the discount and then say, "I still want to think about it." Your story has to show that this isn't going to be easy: the manager might say no regardless of how perfect the prospect is. And if the manager does make this one-time exception, it would look really bad for the sales rep if the prospect didn't buy. All of this just emphasizes that the rep and the prospect are on the same team. When you plant the idea that you're going out on a limb for the prospect, they're more likely to make that commitment. It's the principle of reciprocation at work.

There are three possible responses the prospect could have to this question.

1. "Tell them I still need time to think, no matter what."
2. "If the discount is good enough, we have a deal."
3. "How big a discount are we talking about?"

Option 1 is a red light. You'd politely tell them that if they aren't able to move forward at any price point, you'll hold off going to your manager. There's no sense making a big case if the prospect isn't ready to commit. When they're prepared to give that green light (if the price is right), then you'll talk to the manager. Leave that bullet in the chamber and use it as a way to follow up with them. This answer also indicates they aren't 100 percent sold on things and you might have to go back to square one.

Option 2 is an obvious green light. You'd put them on hold or perhaps even call them back. In that two- or three-minute break, the prospect is waiting to hear if the manager approved the discount. The rep can't just pick up and say, "Great news, here's the new price." If it were that easy, it would sound suspicious. The rep needs to use that time to consider how they're going to present the story of persuading the manager. Of course, everything in that story is another opportunity to recap the reasons the product is a great fit for that prospect. Then you tell them the discounted price and review why this would be such a strong ROI for them.

Option 3 is a yellow light, but you'd proceed much the same way you would with option 2. You can respond with:

Sales Rep: I am not sure, but I will do my best to see if he/she can approve some type of floor pricing. Assuming it was a discount that you were happy with, you would move forward with us, correct?

You are getting right back into getting that green light. They might just need a better case made for their ROI, or they might need one more shot before they're ready to buy. Because in reality, the discount you offer would not be the lowest price possible. You have one more bullet in your chamber. If the discount doesn't close the prospect and they want more time to think, you can have the sales manager follow up with them directly and offer them a custom price that's even lower.

Bear in mind, a discount may be your last bullet, but it isn't a magic bullet. Slashing the price isn't going to save you from a bad pitch. You still need to make all your points along the way and earn their business. If the prospect doesn't believe in the value of your product or that it will solve their problems, it doesn't matter how low the price is. The discount only works when price is the only objection a prospect has left.

TRANSITION TO CLOSE FROM DISCOUNT

Once you have the discount ready, you need to present it to the prospect. This is often where amateur reps rush into things, create shortcuts, and ultimately still end up with no deal. Let's say you are calling the prospect back. When the prospect answers the phone, here is what you *don't* want to say:

Sales Rep: Hi, **[PROSPECT NAME]**, this is Butch over at Sales Lab Scripting. So I have great news. I talked to my manager, and he approved a great discount for you. I got your monthly price down by a hundred dollars. So if everything sounds good, I can go ahead and get you started. What do you think?

There are several things wrong with this. Amateur reps tend to just jump right out of the gates with the discount. We aren't ready for that yet. There are a few steps we need to take here. These steps can also be used by a manager calling the prospect back on behalf of the rep to present the discount and go for the close.

STEP 1: RECAP

Sales Rep: Hi, **[PROSPECT NAME]**, this is Butch over at Sales Lab Scripting. All right, so I did speak with my manager, and I have a few things to go over with you if now is a good time? Okay, great, so when I spoke to **[MANAGER NAME]**, I told him/her we were at **[CURRENT PRICING AND PACKAGE]**. I told him/her I felt if we did something out of the ordinary for you on pricing, you would move forward with us.

STEP 2: BUILDUP

Sales Rep: I mentioned exactly why you would be the perfect fit for our product. **[RECAP THOSE VALUE POINTS AND CURRENT PAIN POINTS.]** I also mentioned that I truly feel the hardest part here is just getting your foot in the door and that if we could do something on our end to get you on the platform, once you are using it, you will fall in love with the product and be blown away with the results. I also told him/her that if we overperformed for you, you would be happy to spend more money with us and you would be a huge advocate for us in the future.

STEP 3: DISCOUNT THEN TRANSITION TO CLOSE

Sales Rep: So here is what we came up with: we are going to apply a lifetime discount of **[INSERT DISCOUNT]** to your account. This allows an easier transition to our platform and gets your foot in the door. This gets you to our floor pricing and is such great value for everything we are doing. Think about this; it doesn't take much for you to see a great ROI at this price, not to mention how much better this product will be across the board than what you're working with now.

For this discount, my manager has asked if you could do two things. First, if you could please not mention this discount to others as this specialty pricing isn't something we can do for everyone. Second, once we perform highly for you, if you could be an advocate for us and speak highly of us to others whenever you get the chance. Just like your business, we can grow ours through word of mouth, and that is where we will benefit from this in the long run.

So, with your greenlight, **[THEIR NAME]**, all we need to do from here is schedule your onboarding, and I will also get that initial invoice sent over. Did you want me to send it to **[THEIR EMAIL]**?

Let's break down what we did here. In Step 1, we ask the question "Is now a good time?" The reason for this is that we want their undivided attention, and we are going to be going for the close at the end of this conversation. Keep in mind we are asking this right after we mention we have spoken to our manager. So the prospect knows they need to stick around to hear the discount. If they say, "No, it is not a good time," we schedule a callback when they have a few minutes. If they say yes, we have their permission not only to recap the discount but to assume the sale.

In Step 2, we take one more opportunity to mention the

reasons they need help solving these business problems and why our product is the perfect solution, all while putting an image in their head of the product exceeding their expectations.

In Step 3, we jump into the discount, reminding them how they can justify the newly discounted price because it is outweighed by the value they are going to get from the services delivered. We then legitimize the discount by asking them not to share pricing and reminding them of the way the deal will benefit our company in the future. We don't stop, nor do we ask them what they think. We are going for the soft close, once again referencing "green light" and jumping into what our next steps would be. The email confirmation acts as our trial close. Getting them to say yes to confirming a correct email address is easier than getting a yes to signing up for something, even though they mean the same thing.

SECOND VOICE

With everything we have mentioned so far on closing, sometimes no matter what is said, a second voice, especially one of authority, is needed to close the sale. We have seen *many reps* fail despite sticking to a solid script, but when the manager repeats the same things said by the rep, the prospect agrees to purchase. Managers should be actively aware of or involved in as many closings as possible.

CALLING BACK

No matter how great of a "closer" you are, deals won't always close on the demo, and a follow-up may be required. When you're going back and forth on the phone with a prospect, there are times you should continue fighting to make the sale today, and there are times you should quit for the day and call the person back later. If a prospect is allowing you to rebut and go back and forth with them, you need to do everything you can to make the sale that day. But if you've tried multiple angles and have gone several rounds trying to get the prospect to purchase today, and you feel a shift in their tone and demeanor where they are starting to get frustrated with you, it may be time to pack it in. When this happens, you need to make sure you set yourself up for success on the next call.

Our golden rule on follow-ups is email as little as possible! Instead, what you want to do is set up a very specific time and date for a callback and final answer, preferably within the week. If they email you additional questions or concerns, don't waste time typing everything out and sending it to them. You have lost control at that point, and you have no idea when they will read that email or respond. Instead, always opt for calling them or setting up a time for a quick call so you can speak with them to address their email. And when you do call them back, have a specific plan in place. Do not just say, "Hey, so what'd you think? Have you come to a decision yet?" Instead, you want to politely greet them, recap some of their favorite parts of the presentation, remind them of any incentives you gave them, and then ask them for their business.

CHAPTER 5

DOING THE RESEARCH

Now that you understand how the basic script templates work, it's time to uncover all the information you need to fill in the blanks and create custom scripts for your product and business. Then those first-draft scripts must be tested and developed in real-world situations. Finally, you need to identify and equip the right person (if it's not you) to put those steps into action: your "script master."

To prepare your Call 1 script, you need to develop your thirty-second pitch. You're looking for the best and most succinct way to explain your product and set yourself apart from the competition. For your Call 2 script, you need to know how to customize it to demonstrate your product while also proactively addressing your prospects' most important concerns. Whether you're developing a script for yourself or your team or you're a leader who will delegate the work, it all starts with research.

KNOWING YOUR PRODUCT, PROSPECTS, AND COMPETITORS

To do proper research, you need to understand what is most important to your prospects and how your product helps them. What services do they offer, and which ones are the most profitable or preferred? What are their goals? Do they want to grow their businesses, save themselves time and money, or reduce stress and hassle? What are their most common problems, and what issues does the product solve for them? Can the product do something they never even knew was an option? Are they putting up with unseen limitations in their current solution that you could improve? What are their major cost drivers, and what risks do they need to mitigate?

In order to present yourself as an industry expert, you need to understand industry terminology. Whether the prospect is a home appraiser or an attorney, be certain you understand the lingo of the industry so you can use it appropriately. For example, to pitch software to real estate photographers, you might ask how many team members they have out in the field and whether they have different skill levels, then throw in a question about how many of them have their Part 107. That's the license to fly a drone, and someone would have to really know the industry to ask about it. That immediately positions you as the prospect's equal. Any insider knowledge specific to the prospect's line of work is going to elevate the rep's professional credibility. The best compliment a rep can get is to be asked by a prospect if they were ever in the business themselves.

When it comes to your competition, you need to be very familiar with the products you're pitching against. You need to know what the competition offers and how your product is different and better to build all those points of contrast into the script. You can glean information from listening to calls from the sales floor, asking your data team, taking good notes on customer calls, and doing independent research on competitor companies.

To get you started on the correct path, here are some sample topics and questions you'll want to understand (notice that many overlap):

YOUR PRODUCT

- What exactly can your product do?
- What problems does your product solve for your prospects?
- What features do your prospects love that are unique to your product?
- What features of your product don't get a strong response from your prospects?
- Which pitches for your product get the most consistently positive responses?

YOUR PROSPECT

- What are your prospect's day-to-day responsibilities, and what are the details of the work they do?
- What lingo does your prospect use?
- What is their opportunity cost/loss by not using your product?
- What are your prospect's most common objections?
- What are the most common rebuttals that overcome those objections?
- What does your prospect love about your product?

YOUR COMPETITOR

- What exactly does your competitor offer?
- How much does it cost? What is their pricing model?
- How does your product differ from your competitor's?
- What do your prospects like about your competitor's product?
- What do your prospects not like about your competitor's product?
- What's the best way to differentiate your product from your competitor's?
- How can you find out which product your prospect is using?

RESEARCH METHODS

You need very different kinds of information to create your script for Call 1 than you do to write your script for Call 2, so you should use a variety of research methods. Call 1 requires you to write a quick pitch. So much of that research can be done just by listening to phone calls and interviewing top sales reps and leaders in your company. However, when you're researching for Call 2, you're building a substantive presentation. You need a broader base of information, so you should bring in relevant insights about your product, customers, and competitors from the experts on those topics: your product people, customer support team, and maybe even leadership, like the CEO.

CALL ANALYSIS

The first step in researching your new script is analyzing what's currently happening on the phones. That entails making and reviewing calls and listening to other people's calls.

If your company already has prerecorded calls, you'll want

to listen to the top reps setting appointments and closing sales. You should also listen to calls that *don't* set appointments or close. Listening to calls with a wide variety of outcomes will give you crucial information about what approaches work consistently, what your customers respond to, and what they don't. Don't just get excited because one line in one call worked well. Look for recurring, predictable patterns. The important thing is to collect successful pitches and find the common elements among them.

As far as how many to listen to—that depends on what stage your company is in and the caliber of reps you're listening to. A good rule of thumb is the more calls, the better. Five hundred calls is better than one hundred. And one hundred calls is better than twenty. Listen to enough calls that you're confident the patterns you recognize are in fact patterns and not just one-offs.

INTERVIEWS

The second research method uses recorded interviews and employee role-playing to ask the questions we provided earlier in the chapter. Top sales reps and managers are often the most helpful. They understand the product and also the benefits for the customer. The important thing to remember is to look at the whole picture but take each individual piece of information with a grain of salt. You're trying to find consistent patterns between the different reps and managers. If they're all saying the same things work for them, it's likely a worthwhile pattern to explore. If they each say something different works, it's likely each solution is unique to one employee, and it might be that none is scalable.

If possible, a great person to interview is the most knowledgeable and passionate about the product and the company:

the CEO, especially if the CEO is sales-minded. They've had to give their own version of a thirty-second pitch hundreds of times, and they've had to dive deep into the product when giving presentations to board members and investors. The CEO can be a great resource if they have the time to meet with you.

A.J.'s experience at a real estate startup is a great example of performing research based on interviews. The company provided leads of potential home buyers to mortgage lenders. He was tasked with creating call scripts and building out a brand-new team from zero to more than twenty sales reps.

First, he asked the CEO to share every recorded call he had where he pitched the product himself. He only had a few. So, to supplement that material, A.J. asked him to role-play and pitch the product in thirty seconds as if A.J. were a busy mortgage lender. The CEO quickly explained the product and benefits, A.J. threw out questions and objections for him to answer, and they recorded the conversation. Afterward, A.J. reviewed and transcribed the recording to fit the pitch and rebuttals into a cold-call script template.

With that solid base, A.J. got a list of prospects and began cold-calling. It was clunky and long at first. Every day, he reviewed the day's calls, isolated the prospects' objections, created responses, asked the CEO how he'd handle those objections, and tested out his answers. After days of refining through trial and error, A.J. eventually had a well-oiled pitch and was setting appointments at a high rate.

Next came the demo. A.J. asked the CEO for any presentations he'd given about the product—to lenders, investors, anyone. Again they recorded role-plays, and A.J. went through the exact same process he did for the cold-call script, transcribing everything into the demo templates. This time, as you can imagine, it was more time-consuming and required more than just speaking to the CEO. For in-depth product knowledge and questions, he interviewed the product team. To understand prospect concerns and needs, he interviewed the prospect service team. After several recorded interviews, A.J. had enough information to input into the Call 2 guide. And just like he did with Call 1, he used trial and error to refine his pitch. It went from clunky and long to effective and efficient. That's what you want to do.

During these interviews, discernment is key. Product people can help you learn to explain how a product works. However, product people can sometimes get in the weeds and provide too much information—what we call "information overload." Remember, your prospect cares more about the benefits than they do the features, so you need to strike a good balance between explaining how the features work and demonstrating and doubling down on the benefits.

Interviewing customer service people can also be tricky, but a lot of great information can be gleaned if you are selective. They know very well what customers like and dislike about your product because they hear every customer compliment and complaint lodged after the sales rep makes the sale. (That also means they know which agents on your team set proper expectations and which ones don't.) They can help you understand the customer onboarding process so you can walk the prospect seamlessly into it. That said, choosing the *right* information from customer support is where the art is. Customer service reps may downplay the product's capabilities to minimize customer expectations and reduce complaints. Low expectations might translate to less-demanding customers, but they might not be great for selling your product. Remember, you want to write a script that sells your product at a fast clip while simultaneously maximizing retention—that's a delicate balance.

If you already have comprehensive knowledge of your customers and competitors, it may not be necessary to start research completely from scratch. But if you're developing a new customer vertical or trying to crack a vertical that hasn't responded well in the past, a comprehensive research period can be very useful.

> The sample scripts in Chapters 2 and 3 contain sections to fill in with the results of your research.

THE DEVELOPMENT PROCESS

The lengths of your two call scripts will obviously vary greatly. For Call 1, your script should really only be three to five minutes long from start to finish when read out loud with no interruptions. Of course, in practice, that time might triple depending on whether you're dealing with an A, B, or F Prospect, whether it's an inbound or outbound call, and the complexity of your product. For Call 2, your script will probably have a read time anywhere from twenty to thirty minutes with no interruptions. And like with Call 1, that time could triple depending on the prospect, type of call, and product. Think of your call scripts like your car's navigation. If you have smooth roads and no traffic, the drive might only be thirty minutes. But if you catch rush hour traffic and a bunch of angry drivers, that same drive might take ninety minutes.

Testing and validating your draft script *looks* like pitching prospects on the phone. In reality, this stage is less concerned with closing individual sales than with collecting information. For example, you might need to spend time asking questions you normally wouldn't (in case you need that knowledge to sell better to prospects like them in the future).

Throughout this development phase, it's very important you aren't attached to the outcome of each individual call. If you are too caught up in selling every prospect, you won't be listening and capturing the building blocks of your script. During this phase, you have to be focused on long-term gains, not short-term wins.

For Call 1, you'll usually face universal behavioral objections like "I'm busy" or "No thank you, not interested." Each of these objections will have standard rebuttals. You'll also hear a few objections specific to your industry or competition, and your research and development will reveal which rebuttals are most effective.

The same holds true for your Call 2 script. There will be universal behavioral objections that have standard rebuttals, like "I need to discuss this with my partner," and others that will be product- or industry-specific and need customized rebuttals. Gathering objections on Call 2 is pretty easy because if you haven't anticipated them in your call script, you'll hear a flurry of them when you get to the end of the demo. You should write down each one so they can be proactively addressed in the demo script. Any door that can't be closed early needs a rebuttal crafted for the end of the script. Each demo during development is a learning opportunity. Michelangelo used to say he created sculptures by chipping away everything that didn't belong. You are doing the same—chipping away all the unnecessary words and thoughts so the shape of an ideal script can emerge.

With a development mindset focused on learning rather than selling, you (or the person leading your research) need to spend at least 80 percent of your time on the phone, making calls. Success in this process comes from repetition, and the more prospects you speak with, the quicker you will make progress. As a matter of fact, someone who is willing to devote 100 percent of their nine-to-five time to calling and experimenting with scripts is going to be far more successful. They can't talk to prospects at ten o'clock at night, but they can devote time off the clock to writing and script building. As time progresses and you start to narrow down your pitch, you can spend more and more time analyzing calls versus making dials yourself.

RESOURCES FOR RESEARCH

The research and development process will be most effective with support from company leadership, including providing specific tools, resources, and incentives. If you're a sales rep working independently, you may not get extra resources provided by your company during the workweek. But the payoff of having a consistent pitch that provides top results is more than worth the time you spend working on it after hours.

First, you need a phone-recording system that makes it easy to retrieve and study calls. Ideally, it would be integrated with a customer relationship management (CRM) system that can track dials, pitches, appointment sets, holds, and sales (so you know which calls are worth reviewing and why).

If you're looking for a CRM system, we recommend Sellfire, the purpose-built, complete solution to inside sales.

Next, you need a source for leads. Some sales reps prefer to source their own leads because they believe they are more successful when they research each prospect they call, study their websites, and have control over which lead to pursue. From our experience, that's a holdover from high-touch enterprise sales, and it isn't necessary or helpful within a scripted process.

Randomly searching potential prospects online and manually dialing them one by one isn't an efficient use of your time and will make your research and development process drag on far too long. Preferably, you'd have a data operations person create a database with business information and phone numbers so you (and your reps) can move quickly from one prospect to the next. If your company doesn't have a dedicated, full-time data operations person, consider assigning someone to support your sales team by creating prospect lists for them.

FIND YOUR SCRIPT MASTER

We've done all the hard work for you in figuring out the best strategies for structuring a pitch, word patterns, and tonality. If you're not writing the script for yourself or your team, now you need to find someone who will creatively and effectively customize those templates with your business information. There's a certain set of traits and skills required to be a script master:

- They need to have a very high sales IQ. Your script master needs to be a strong salesperson with consistently high performance.
- They need a consistent pitch so they're saying nearly the same thing to every prospect. If you listened to ten of their calls, they'd all sound generally the same. Whether they realize it or not, they've honed that pitch over time because it works, and they're confident in pitching it exactly that way.
- They need an analytical mindset. They need to be able to listen to a large number of calls, break them down, and understand what went right, what went wrong, and why.
- They need to be a big-picture thinker motivated by being

tied to the future success of the company, not just their own personal success.

- They must also be humble, dedicated, and diligent enough to study this playbook and follow it precisely. The strategies and philosophies in this book are crucial to creating powerful scripts, so they need to understand and apply them.
- They need a disciplined and determined mindset. We've made script writing simple with our scripts and guides, but that doesn't mean it's easy. It requires a lot of trial and error to get everything right, and you may receive resistance from others and even yourself at times, so you need to persevere through frustration and stay focused on the bigger goal without slacking off or giving up when things get tough.

Your script master will be leading your sales lab and will most likely become a significant leader in your organization in the future, so they also need leadership qualities. Those include high emotional intelligence, humility, a willingness to learn, empathy, and strong coaching skills.

You may not be confident that you can identify the right script master—one may not even exist on your team yet. Don't panic. It's a rare mix of skills, and most companies don't have someone on their team who checks all these boxes. A good candidate can grow into the role. You can find more resources for recruiting or developing a script master on our website, www.Sellfire.com/SalesLabScripting.

When you approach a potential script master, you need to frame the project correctly and set the right expectations. Explain to them that your goal is to scale your sales operations by hiring new reps based on their attitudes and work ethics. You're looking for coachable, hardworking, positive people, and you need to equip them with a script and process that allow the company to scale.

Give the script master this playbook so they can understand how the scripting process should work and you'll have shared terminology to discuss your plans and let them know you're trusting them to use it. Your script master needs to be humble and teachable enough to follow the process. A sales rep with a big ego will want to figure everything out for themselves. That's not the right pick for this role. They can't bring their ego into this exercise. You want someone who can use their sales skills for the research and development phase but is also humble enough to be excited about a step-by-step plan to help them be successful.

THE SCRIPT MASTER'S OUTLOOK

Your script master needs to be tied to the company's future success. They need a motivating factor to make the process work. Typically that's established through commissions, stock, and equity that align their interests with the company's. You can also establish performance goals for the sales lab team based on their ability to increase the company's revenue.

However you choose to reward your script master, what matters is they are brought into the big picture. Leading change and acquiring the skills to run a sales lab is going to be a fantastic opportunity for their career. If they succeed in mastering this scripting process, positive things are going to happen for your company and for the script master personally.

Once they build and roll out a set of winning scripts, they aren't going to go back on the floor full time as a regular sales rep. They will be on a leadership track, either managing teams or perhaps partnering with an existing leader to oversee sales performance. They'll be training the rest of the sales force, reinforcing the system, and helping scale it as you hire. Your success will be their success and vice versa.

Some excellent sales reps don't have any interest in leadership, coaching, or managing because they don't want the extra responsibilities or longer hours. You want to make sure the script master is up for the journey.

ARE YOU THE SCRIPT MASTER?

If you're a rep or a sales manager and you want to become a sales lab script master, you should hand this book to your boss or CEO. If they want to improve their business, they'll invest time and resources into helping you. If they won't and you want to go at it on your own and prove it yourself first, you'll need to put the time in to do your own research on your own time.

The same way we study to create the perfect pitch, you can study the highest performers in your company. Don't just try to imitate them—you'll tank. Analyze them. Look for the common patterns that always work. Figure out why. Then you can use our call script structures and templates to fill that information into the blanks.

When your performance goes up exponentially and you're crushing your goals week after week and month after month, people will notice. They're going to want to know what you're doing so they can replicate it.

That's when you hand them this book again and say, "I told you so."

Once company leadership understands how this process is fueling your success and its potential to transform results across the whole sales team, you won't have to convince anyone of anything anymore. The results will speak for themselves.

PUTTING RESEARCH INTO ACTION

The script master's analysis is deep, but if done correctly, it doesn't take long. For the first few days, the script master should be interviewing reps; listening to calls; talking to upper management, client services, or the product team; researching competitors online; and (mostly) making development calls. Within the first week, they should have an initial draft script for Call 1 that they can test, tweak, and refine. It's a "ready, fire, aim" approach. There's no point having the script master prepare a script on paper that doesn't work in real life. By the second or third week, Call 1 should be improved, and the script master should start working on Call 2. During the next few weeks, they should work on optimizing both scripts.

Everyone's situation is unique, so the timing recommended here might vary. But if your script master is dedicating all their time to this process, they should have both Call 1 and Call 2 scripts built within the first few weeks and ready for the next stage of development by the sales lab team. You want to make sure you're getting enough data, so your lab should run for at least sixty days for further refinement. After being used for a month or two on the phone and being confirmed statistically significant improvement, your scripts should be refined enough to roll out.

Now that the research is done and the development process is underway, let's look at what you need to do to build your sales lab and start testing.

CHAPTER 6

BUILDING YOUR SALES LAB

Now that your script master has developed well-researched draft call scripts, you'll assemble a small team of sales reps to act as researchers and put your scripts to the test under the script master's direction and management.

So, if your script master based the scripts on your top performer and tested which portions were repeatable, why do you need the sales lab at all? Hasn't the script master already proven the scripts work?

Absolutely not! The script master has proven the scripts work *for them*. Now we need to make sure they work for the rest of the team and the floor. Remember, the purpose of the sales lab is to produce scripts that will *scale*.

As your team tests the scripts on real prospects, they'll keep track of recurring problems or objections so they can analyze them and update the scripts to proactively eliminate or overcome them. In this chapter, we'll cover:

- How to choose the right members for your research team
- What rules you should establish for working in the lab

- Which prospects the lab should target
- What data you need to track and analyze
- How to coach team members during the testing phase
- How to address common problems that may come up
- When and how to incorporate changes into the scripts
- How to know when your scripts are ready to roll out to the rest of the sales floor

WHO BELONGS ON YOUR TEAM

Are you an individual sales rep planning to upgrade your performance with scripting? Take some time for self-reflection. Do you have the following qualities yourself? Are you willing to develop them?

Choosing the right team members and setting up the right rules for running the lab are critical. In fact, the way you choose your team members will set your hiring criteria going forward. As we mentioned in Chapter 1, our methodology changes the way you hire and manage sales reps. Instead of looking for reps with a lot of prior experience and rock-star performance, you'll look for qualities that make for a good sales rep in a scripted system. We call these qualities "the big three."

The first is a **positive attitude**. As you know, this type of selling is not easy, and there is a lot of rejection in high-velocity sales, especially when you're testing and learning a new script. A glass-half-full attitude in this environment is vital because it boosts team morale and contributes to a more resilient and solution-oriented approach to overcoming new challenges. This trait is vital for not only sales lab members but also the entire sales floor once you prove the concept and transition the team over. So make sure you're choosing those on the team who have a track record and history of having and keeping a positive attitude.

The second is **being a hard worker**. On a scripted, high-velocity sales team, lazy sales reps almost always get weeded out. They don't hit their targets and are often lazy in other parts of the business, like staying on script. Hard workers, on the other hand, are usually reliable, and you can count on them showing up every day. Additionally, they learn more quickly through repetition, and if coached correctly on a well-written script, their hard work will almost always pay off. So when selecting reps, make sure you're choosing ones with a track record and history of working hard and putting in a lot of effort.

The third and final attribute of "the big three" is **being coachable**. Having coachable sales reps on your team is essential because they are receptive to using the script, receptive to your feedback, and continuously eager to improve. When you have reps that are coachable and quick learners, it leads to faster skills development, quicker adoption of the script and company changes, and ultimately an increase in early sales success. So when choosing reps for your lab, choose the ones who have proven they are receptive to feedback and quick to implement it.

A quick story to learn from: In one of A.J.'s labs, the team fell into the trap of including a top sales rep who was a great closer. Although they knew he'd make sales as a naturally talented rep, his ego was overinflated, and it got in the way of his effectiveness as a lab member. He said he'd be on script during the interview process, but when it came time to be on the phone, he prioritized his selling style and closing skills over staying on script. He completely missed the point of doing the lab at all and wound up getting kicked off the team after just a few days. Don't make the mistake of thinking the best sales reps are necessarily the right ones for your sales lab team.

TEAM MAKEUP

Your lab team should have enough members to generate plenty of data but not so many it threatens team cohesion or becomes hard to manage. We recommend lab teams of between six and ten reps. If your sales force is too small to dedicate that many reps, the minimum would be three or four. If your company is very large, we recommend cutting off at twelve to fifteen team members. A team larger than that becomes unwieldy.

Additionally, your team needs to represent the average performance of your sales force, so you should choose members with *different levels of skill and experience.* You want a mix of good performers, average performers, and brand-new or underperforming reps. This experiment is intended to produce a script that will work for everyone, so every skill level needs to be represented. Your goal is to see consistent growth across the board. Mixing up your team also helps prove the system makes sense for your company. When the whole team starts to make amazing gains, skeptics won't be able to argue the team was stacked. The results will speak for themselves.

MAKE IT SPECIAL

Joining the sales lab is a privilege because those reps will be in on the ground floor of the company's new direction. Not only will they have the opportunity to work closely with the script master who will coach and mentor them, they will have input into polishing the scripts that the rest of the company will eventually use. The whole point of this system is to dramatically improve sales performance, so each rep can anticipate a big increase in their commissions once the scripts are tuned properly. They'll have a massive advantage over the other reps when the scripts roll out because their performance will already be optimized. The sales lab can seed your future leaders in the company. You should interview and handpick these team members carefully.

Beyond "the big three," your sales lab members also need to demonstrate the following qualities:

- Reliability
- Advocacy
- Commitment

Reliability: We mentioned this earlier as a subset of being a hard worker. The sales lab is only going to run for a short time, perhaps one to three months. In that time, you need to collect data on as many calls as possible. Everyone needs to be present, on time, and dialing every day. A prospective member's attendance needs to be consistently excellent. A track record of Monday morning "Must be something I ate" call-ins isn't going to cut it. Each rep's planned time off also matters. If they're going to miss any significant amount of time during the lab period, it will hamper the results. They may be a great team player the rest of the year, but if they miss out on training or brainstorming sessions during the lab, there's no practical way to catch them up. Often reps who really understand the opportunity the lab opens up for them will offer to reschedule their time off if possible. They don't want to miss out. Make sure you choose reps who have a solid history of being on time and not missing work often.

Advocacy: Your lab members will become advocates for the system and scripts they help develop, so they need to show enthusiasm and the ability to inspire others. Your lab team will work separately from the rest of the sales force, but they aren't in a bubble. Their peers on the sales floor will be curious about the project and want to know how it's going, both in terms of results and the members' experiences. They aren't going to ask managers—they'll ask their friends and colleagues to get an inside view. You want to choose team members who will be good representatives for the system and the new direction of the company. Members who are good ambassadors for the system build credibility and make rollout go much more smoothly. Their ability to advocate and build positive anticipation for the rollout can set them up as leaders in the future.

Committed: Lastly, lab members need to show they are committed to the experimental process and the long-term success of the system. We recommend the script master draw up a commitment agreement for the lab members that outlines their expectations and responsibilities and have them sign and date it. If the individual or lab as a whole hits a rough patch, that contract can be a good tool to redirect members to stay on script, stay focused and consistent, and help bring the experiment back on track.

A TWO-WAY STREET

Creating a sales lab is a significant commitment in both directions. The members of the lab must commit to following the rules so the experiment is valid and useful. The company's leaders must also commit time, energy, and resources to making it work.

COMMITMENT FROM THE TEAM

Sales reps who are chosen to join the lab team should commit to following the experimental protocol precisely and consistently. This process will be laid out in a few clear rules and documented in the contract written up by the script master.

There are four fundamental rules we always include:

1. **Stay on script.** They can't test the script if they aren't actually using the words and tonality handed to them. They're looking for data points, and going off script ruins the data and undermines the whole purpose of the lab. They are not working in the lab to improve their individual performance but to generate data for analysis. If they go off script, their calls are useless for the purposes of the lab. They need to see themselves as scientists conducting experiments with the formulas and ingredients listed in the test. If they start bringing in other factors, it'll skew the results of the data.

2. **You are not a teacher.** Everyone likes to feel knowledgeable and helpful, so it's very common for an average or below-average performer to try to "help" by coaching new hires. This is detrimental to the experimental process. Team members should focus on learning the script, not trying to teach others. The team already has a manager, and everyone needs to focus on doing their own job. The one exception to this rule would be situations where one rep hears another going off script and reminds them to get back on. Let the script master (and the script itself) do the rest.

3. **Work hard every day.** Every rep needs to be fully committed to showing up physically and mentally. They need to meet their dialing and talk-time minimums. The minimums for each team will depend on a number of factors, like whether or not reps have to research their own leads, whether they are only running Call 1 or they are also running demo calls, and, if so, how many demos they might have in a day. The script master should set realistic targets for their lab members and hold them accountable.

4. **Practice deliberately.** A lot of people work hard but aren't

successful. Successful people work hard, but they also work smart. If they come across a challenge, they identify it and diligently test ways to overcome it. They don't just try to outwork the problem and keep banging their head against the same wall. They write down the objections they hear, think about why those objections have come up, and work with the script master to test a new solution to their problems. If it works, they move on to the next challenge. If it doesn't work, they report back and collaborate on a new solution. They are always optimizing and getting better at what they do. Deliberate practice, coined by Geoff Colvin in his book *Talent Is Overrated*, helps individual lab members, and their recordings help the script master discover strengths and weaknesses in the script.

In addition to the contract, we recommend the team create a team name and motto to express their mission. It's a great exercise to do in training because it helps the team come together and motivate each other. Posting the motto where everyone can see it becomes a point of pride and emphasizes the team's uniqueness.

COMMITMENT TO THE TEAM

Company leadership must also make some commitments to the lab team in order for the experiment to be successful. First and foremost, the company must be fully committed to implementing the system across the board. Your recruitment of lab members will rely heavily on their future prospects within the company. If you tell them they're going to have an advantage after the rollout, getting in on the ground floor, and positioning themselves as future sales leaders, you have to make good.

You're picking the hardest-working, most enthusiastic people for the team. If you frustrate them by being half-hearted or you don't keep your promises, you'll lose good people.

Compensation

You must also commit to supporting the experiment with some temporary changes to the lab members' compensation structure. They're going to be off the phones in training and then testing unproven scripts. There's always a risk their sales numbers could go down in the short term, before the script is optimized.

Instead of a standard salary-plus-commission structure, offer a guaranteed minimum that will let them stand pat for the month or two of lab time. Typically, we look at each rep's historical average over the last six months and set that as their baseline. For new reps without much history, we take their salary as the baseline. The point is if you want good people in the lab, you need to ensure they don't lose out financially during the testing phase. Of course, alongside those guarantees, you have their commitment to work hard and keep up their minimums. If they don't live up to their responsibilities, they are removed from the lab and go back to the regular sales floor.

Technology

Your script master will need to listen to the team's calls to break them down and give feedback as well as observe what is or is not working in the script. Most sales teams already have some kind of system to support call monitoring and recording, but we've found that often our clients aren't using it frequently enough or tapping into its full potential. The script master (and every sales manager as you roll the system out) must devote a significant amount of time every day to reviewing and analyzing calls with standardized Call Breakdown Sheets so they can provide feedback to the team as a group and to individuals in a one-on-one setting. In addition to call recording, we recommend a two-way system that allows the script master (and sales managers) to hear a call live and coach the rep behind the scenes.

We also recommend a lead-distribution system to help SDRs or reps in general move quickly from one call to the next. Some companies still expect reps to source their own leads and add each customer's data to the CRM database. That's far less efficient and can make the testing phase drag out longer than it should. You need a critical mass of calls in order to gather enough data and draw valid conclusions. The quicker your reps can run those calls, the quicker they will ramp up their learning curve and the quicker your lab can polish the call scripts. Bear in mind, you want the sales lab to be as representative as possible of normal operations on the floor. If you mess with too many variables (like the way they source leads), it could end up affecting key performance indicators (KPIs) and screwing up the data for the sales lab.

Recognition

One of the most important resources company leadership can offer to your lab team is the time and a budget to recognize their efforts and successes. Phone sales can be challenging, even with a good script, and the team's hard work should be appreciated. Your lab team in particular should be able to enjoy coming to work every day because they are part of a unique, dedicated group working on the cutting edge of the company's future. In every sales lab we've run, there's been a sense of mission. People were excited to be part of something that could dramatically change the company. The sales lab team can take pride in creating something special.

Your script master should have the resources to run contests, set incentives, and give awards to reps who hit their goals and make a positive impact on the team. When your lab members know they're doing a good job and their work is appreciated, they have more fun and stay motivated.

COACHING YOUR LAB TEAM

As the resident expert on scripting, your script master will train and manage the lab team. As the coach, their work will include:

- Introducing the system to reps
- Setting daily and weekly patterns of brainstorming, practice, and review
- Setting goals and tracking KPIs for the team
- Reviewing calls and breaking them down for analysis
- Prioritizing feedback to address the most urgent issues first
- Tweaking and updating the scripts as needed

INTRODUCING THE SCRIPTS

When we create sales labs for clients, we encounter reps with two different backgrounds: people who have never used a script at all and people who have used a suggested script as a guide. Both types need to be educated on how our system works and what they're really trying to do in the sales lab. People who have never used a script at all are invariably easier to coach. They don't have any preconceived notions or bad habits to unlearn. As soon as they get the script, they tend to assume they are supposed to read it word for word.

Reps who are in the habit of using a script as a general guideline can have a hard time getting used to our system. They have an ingrained expectation that it's all right to deviate from the script, skip around, and make changes on the fly. The script master must impress on this group how vital it is to stay on script with their words and tonality.

Nobody responds well to being micromanaged, so the script master needs to explain that the script must be followed exactly to get a clear and useful result from the experiment. If you were working in a chemistry lab and you never washed out your beakers, how could you test a new formula? Anything you put into a beaker would become contaminated by whatever unknown substance was in there before. Your scientific process must be precise to be valid.

As part of training the team on the scripts, the script master will introduce a tool that they and the reps can use to help them stay on track—Call Breakdown Sheets. These are little checklists that address everything a rep needs to accomplish in each section and line of the script, such as:

- Did the rep reply right away when the decision maker answered the phone?
- Did the rep read the line word for word without any additions, alterations, or subtractions?
- Did the rep use the right tonality?
- Did the rep sound like a confident, professional expert?

Call Breakdown Sheets allow the script manager to hold the reps accountable and provide detailed feedback on where reps can improve.

> You can find sample Call Breakdown Sheets on our website, www. Sellfire.com/SalesLabScripting.

After training, the lab team will be starting from scratch, so there will be a steep learning curve. No matter how hard you try, they are going to fall off script. Have grace and correct them so they know what to do better next time. It may take them a week or two before they know the scripts and tonality well enough to execute them consistently, and they will continue to improve over time. Even reps who see massive improvement in the first month will typically take up to ninety days to achieve their full potential. The script master will give the reps extremely detailed and granular feedback over the course of the testing phase. The lab members need to understand why precision and consistency matter so they can take that feedback on board and apply it.

> You'll organize training days for lab members in much the same way you'll train the rest of the sales force during rollout. We cover step-by-step training plans in Chapter 7.

ROUTINE FEEDBACK

During the testing phase, the script master should establish regular times to hear feedback or brainstorm solutions with the reps as well as give group and individual coaching. A typical sales team will have regular check-in meetings and individual coaching, but this connection needs to be more frequent and intense in the sales lab.

Every day should start with a team meeting. The group should spend about fifteen minutes considering their goals for the day, reviewing any changes, getting coached on recurring problems, and problem-solving. This can be a good opportunity to identify patterns of objections and come up with new ways to anticipate or rebut them. Then they'll get on the phones for most of the work day.

About thirty or forty-five minutes before close of business, the script master should call the team together. They'll spend that last chunk of the day recapping what the team heard on the phones that day and what the script master observed about their performance. The script master might play an example of someone getting a sale so they can give that rep recognition and team support. These end-of-day meetings should happen daily in the first month of testing and phase out during the second month.

The script master should also have one-on-one meetings with every team member once a week. If a rep is struggling and needs extra coaching, they should meet more often. These regular check-ins give the script master an opportunity to provide individualized feedback, particularly on the rep's weak spots that wouldn't be appropriate to call out in front of the group. Having so many one-on-ones is another reason to keep the lab team small—if there are more than twelve or fifteen people, the script master will have a hard time fitting that many meetings into their week. The script master can also record their feedback on video and send it to a rep if there is a scheduling conflict or they have extra feedback during the week.

CALL BREAKDOWNS

Reviewing performance is essential to deliberate practice. In sports, watching game film is an integral part of a sports team's preparation for game day. It provides a unique perspective and allows players and coaches to analyze past performances;

identify strengths, weaknesses, and patterns; and strategize. Tom Brady, widely regarded as the greatest quarterback in NFL history, is known for his meticulous approach to preparation. Tom would spend countless hours after practice at his house reviewing game and practice film, sometimes sitting for four to five hours straight without getting up from his chair.

Your script master must be just as dedicated to reviewing and analyzing calls on a daily basis to monitor the team's performance and gather insight about the effectiveness of the scripts. They should use the Call Breakdown Sheets introduced in training to check each segment of the call for target behaviors or common errors. This will help ensure every rep is held to the same standard and the scripts are being executed properly. Reps can also use the checklist on their own to improve their practice and help identify areas where they might need help.

So, what should the script master be listening for? *Everything.* There are so many nuances to delivering a script correctly that it can be obvious to a trained listener whether or not a rep will get an appointment (and therefore whether they will eventually get the sale) in the first ten seconds of Call 1—even if they say all the right words. As we discussed in Chapter 2, a strong cold-call script packs an incredible amount of technique into a very short time. That also means a lot of things can go wrong—we've done detailed call breakdowns for clients where a five-minute call generated forty minutes of analysis.

Remember, a successful closing is based on earning "points" along the way, and the points you score at the beginning are the most valuable. Below are some examples of things we look for on a cold call, what we include in our call breakdown guides, and how meticulously we grade our reps:

Here's an example breakdown guide:

1. In the introduction of the call: Did the rep respond in the appropriate time frame when the prospect answered the phone?
   A. No, too long of a pause—0 points
   B. Yes, responded immediately—1 point
2. In the introduction of the call: Did the rep read the words on the script exactly as they're written (no added words, no words left out, no words altered)?
   A. No, there were words added, left out, and/or altered—0 points
   B. Yes, words were said exactly as they were written—1 point
3. In the introduction of the call: Did the rep use the correct tonality (sounded confident, professional, like an expert, etc.)?
   A. No, they didn't sound confident, professional, like an expert—0 points
   B. Yes, they sounded confident, professional, like an expert—1 point
4. In the introduction of the call: Did the rep use the correct timing with their script (not too fast, not too slow, no awkward pauses)?
   A. No, did not use correct timing—0 points
   B. Yes, used correct timing—1 point

And we do this type of meticulous analysis for each section of our scripts (including the thirty-second pitch, confirming the demo, and even the different sections of the demo guide). When you're this meticulous, you can provide precise, scalable, and actionable feedback for a sales rep to improve on.

You can download a sample Call Breakdown Sheet at www.Sellfire. com/SalesLabScripting.

As a word of advice, when doing call breakdowns, managers shouldn't pile on every single thing that went wrong in every coaching session, or the rep will get demoralized and over-whelmed. We recommend only providing a couple things to work on per session (one to three of them). Once you've given the feedback, make sure the rep understands this is what you will be monitoring moving forward and if/when they incorpo-rate the feedback, you will move on to other feedback. You can have the rep sign off on the feedback or not. It's best to check calls the day or two after and have a follow-up meeting three business days later to go over the previous feedback. If they've perfected what needed perfecting, good; move on to new feed-back. If not, have them work on the same feedback. Sometimes it takes time (minutes, days, weeks), so you need to be patient.

Additionally, negative feedback should be paired with praise, recognition, or encouragement—we call this "fire and ice" or a "management sandwich." Even if the rep is struggling in every area, the script master can acknowledge they're work-ing hard and give them hope that they will improve. The most urgent problems should be addressed first—starting with the issues that happened at the very beginning of the call. We can't emphasize this enough: the earlier the rep gets a win or loss, the more weight it carries. Bad habits or recurring issues should be addressed in the order in which they appear in the script.

There's also a natural progression for the reps as they prac-tice. When they start out and haven't mastered the beginning of the cold call, they get hung up on early. They are forced to practice the first part of that script over and over until they get better at it, and then they move on to the next section. When they get good at the second section, the prospect stays on the phone long enough for them to reach the third section, and so forth. It's helpful for the script master to point out this progression because it can encourage new reps to keep working and learning as they go.

When doing group call breakdowns, script masters should also be cautious about which feedback they give to the group and which items they address one-on-one. If only one or two reps are having an issue, that should be dealt with privately. Giving group feedback will likely backfire. Conscientious reps who were already doing things right will get paranoid and overthink their work, or they might resent being corrected on issues they don't have, whereas reps who aren't aware of their mistakes might not recognize themselves and assume the group feedback isn't relevant to them.

We'll talk more about coaching and management in Chapter 8.

UPDATING THE SCRIPT

The purpose of your experiment in the sales lab is to refine your call scripts. However, you can't just tinker with them all the time. Every change you make could have effects on another portion of the call. You must distinguish between problems with execution and problems with the scripts themselves.

First, the script master must ensure the lab team is executing the scripts correctly and consistently. That takes practice, and it's normal for reps to need intensive coaching for the first couple weeks in the lab. Once it's clear from reviewing calls that the scripts are being delivered as they should be, the script master needs to monitor performance for at least a week to see results emerge and allow patterns to develop.

If the script is not producing satisfactory results at that point, it's time to make a change. The script master should consult KPI data and collaborate with the reps to discover recurring problems and address them strategically.

Each element you test must earn its place in the script. If a change or rebuttal works for one sales rep, that's not enough. In a lab of ten to twelve people, you want to see at least three or four reps succeeding with the new language. You need to see that it works consistently before you commit to it. You also need to review calls for consistent delivery. Remember, being on script isn't just about the words on the page but also the rep's tonality. Your sales lab should analyze and refine both.

Each change should run for about a week to see what difference it might make. Obviously, if prospects are having strong negative reactions or getting angry, that's a red flag. That test should stop immediately. Otherwise, as long as performance is improving at a steady rate, the script master should hold the course. Too many changes in rapid succession make it impossible to see what's working and what isn't. Then you're back at square one, like an improvisational seller who doesn't know what's working or why. Changes should be made one at a time and thoroughly tested before anything else gets tweaked or adjusted.

Tracking Your KPIs

Your baseline performance indicators will be determined by your current average performance. That's your control. How much improvement you can expect to see during testing will vary by industry, but you should see statistically significant improvements in all your KPIs (set rate, hold rate, close rate, etc.) as soon as the lab team is executing the scripts consistently. The ultimate indicator of whether your scripts are performing is a binary result. Are you making more money per hour with the scripts: yes or no?

An effective Call 1 script should allow reps to dial far more calls in a day because they aren't wasting time struggling to sell prospects when they're supposed to be focused on setting demos. You should also see a higher set rate for appointments and higher hold rate of prospects keeping appointments. Those will result in running more demos.

An effective Call 2 script will close more demos. When you run a lot more demos and close at a higher rate, you'll see your revenue jump dramatically. You might even increase your average order size, which would increase revenue even without a big jump in your closing rate.

If any of those variables go in the wrong direction—fewer sets, fewer holds, fewer closings—the script needs more work. For example, if your set rate from Call 1 went from 20 percent to 40 percent but your hold rate went from 50 percent down to 20 percent, you'd wind up making less money overall.

Each variable that might go up or down can give you insight into where you need to make changes. The script master should review call recordings to find out how prospects are reacting and what's going wrong. Our model of the thirty-second pitch came from exactly this type of analysis.

Permission to Pitch

Here's a real-world example of putting your data to work to update your script. Our original sales lab didn't use a thirty-second pitch. We developed that later, when our product was used by many different types of businesses across different industries. Our analysis showed that prospects were showing up to the demos at a good rate, and we were closing demos at a very good rate, but we just weren't setting enough appointments.

We looked back at our call dispositions, where the reps label the prospect's response to the cold call, and pulled all the calls where the prospect was flagged as "not interested." When we listened back to those recordings, we found that the reps were getting cut off almost as soon as they introduced themselves. Just a few words in, the contact would say, "Send me an email" or literally "I'm not interested." They weren't even allowing us to pitch.

We came up with a strategy to time-stamp the call before the prospect had a chance to cut us off: a quick thirty-second pitch. Unfortunately, if we jumped right into the pitch, our reps still got cut off. That's when we started asking permission to give the prospect a thirty-second pitch. That convinced more people to hear us out. We were able to build value for the demo. Our set rate from that point forward was much higher.

READY, SET, ROLL OUT

The sales lab should run for roughly one to three months. In some cases, it's immediately clear the scripts are delivering fantastic results and few changes are needed. In other situations, it can take several iterations on the scripts and up to ninety or so days for the reps to ramp up their performance. In most cases, the growth in sales coming out of the lab will make leadership and the rest of the company eager—even impatient—to start using the new system. Once it's clear the scripts are working and the script master has documented all the tonality and best practices that make them work, it's time to roll the system out to the entire sales force. That's what we'll look at in Chapter 7.

ROLLING OUT THE SCRIPT

Rolling out your new sales system means you will bring the results of your work in the sales lab—the polished script, the techniques and rebuttals you prepared, and the final data on the increase in sales performance for the lab team—and present them to the rest of the company. Specifically, you'll teach and explain the method and your scripts to the sales team.

Your rollout plan will reflect the same principles of education and persuasion that you used in crafting your sales scripts. You'll present the benefits and ROI of the new system in a logical way, showing how it is in everyone's best interest. You'll treat the sales team with respect, as intelligent people who can make good choices for themselves. And you'll present the material in a way that anticipates objections or problems and resolves them before they become issues.

In this chapter, we'll cover three phases for rolling out your new system:

- Preparing for rollout
- Training day

- Making the training stick

PREPARING FOR ROLLOUT

As soon as the sales lab starts to show good results, it's time to start preparing for the rollout process. The script master will need at least a few weeks to properly schedule and set up everything they need for training and implementation. Training day will require the sales force to be off the phones all day long (or in a larger company, a team at a time). It needs to be scheduled well in advance.

For companies that work in person (or in a hybrid model with local staff), training day usually happens in a classroom or conference room setting. For fully remote teams (which are becoming more and more prevalent), training can be held in a variety of ways. Some companies hold regular quarterly or biannual conferences. They might set up for three days of meetings in a hotel conference center to build their company culture and community. This can also present a great opportunity to roll out the system as part of a big, fun company-wide event. We've also done some large rollouts remotely, with all the trainees dialing in. Whatever the setting, the basic principles of solid training remain the same.

A successful rollout depends on a solid commitment from company ownership and upper management as well as thorough preparation by the script master. There must be a consistent message from the C-suite on down that the new system is the future of the company. The changes being made go far beyond what individual reps say on the phone.

First, leadership must commit to stability for the existing sales force and management. What you want to avoid is a scenario where you implement a brand-new system, run a sales lab, and train the sales manager and team—only to turn around and immediately lay off the manager and a significant portion of the reps. That's just poor planning and a waste of time. Rolling out this system is a significant investment in your people. Make sure you're investing in people you plan to keep.

The C-suite must champion the system and actively manage the change. They will need to support the script master in setting the right expectations going forward and support sales leaders as they implement the system long-term. A full company-wide rollout will probably involve changes to operations, the compensation structure, and the role of sales managers. Training managers and reps requires time and resources. This change in the sales philosophy is more than procedural—it represents a shift in company culture, and positive cultural change starts from the top.

Change always creates some discomfort and friction, and different people respond to change differently. We've seen a pattern across our client companies that inexperienced and struggling reps are most likely to see scripting as a change for the better. Sales is an intimidating business. Many reps are happy to have clear processes to help them succeed. The highest-performing sales reps tend to be the most skeptical about the new system. After all, their improvisational or loosely scripted approach is working well for them. They often fear a tightly structured script will cramp their style. There can also be an element of ego, where they feel their creativity and talent aren't appreciated.

It's important for both groups to understand that delivering a script correctly and closing sales are an art and a science— they require creativity, salesmanship, and deliberate practice. The script will help them be more consistent and successful, but it doesn't allow them to turn their brains off. They will still need to be attentive, diligent, and fully engaged in order to grow their sales. Managers and leaders must continue to emphasize that the script is a tool. It doesn't do the work by itself.

CHANGES TO COMPENSATION

With a lot of the rollouts we've managed, we've changed the compensation structure to fit the new sales model. A standard model might have a relatively high base salary and fairly modest cap on commissions. Our method is far more advantageous to the sales reps in terms of commissions, so we recommend a plan with a slightly lower base and higher ceiling. Ideally, commissions wouldn't be capped at all. This new structure allows reps who apply themselves and excel with the scripts to reap the benefits of their hard work and attracts applicants who are more competitive than interested in guaranteed security.

From a management perspective, it's not a good idea to rip the Band-Aid off and announce sudden blanket changes to compensation. That's likely to cause a mutiny before the reps even have a chance to understand the advantages of the new system. We typically offer an opt-in period that accompanies the rollout. For example, in the first thirty days after rollout, reps can opt in to the new plan. We're confident the reps who adopt the plan early will see a quick, dramatic increase in their earnings. Of course, that proof of success encourages others to opt in as well.

Once 70 to 80 percent of the sales floor has bought into the new plan, managers can start having conversations with those who continue to hold out. Then it's time to set a deadline when the new plan will become mandatory. Most reps don't take much convincing—their peers will talk about how much more money they're making. Success speaks for itself.

TRAINING MATERIALS

The script master needs to prepare a number of different materials to train managers and reps on the new system. The central element of training will be documents we call the Why Scripts. These are versions of the Call 1 and Call 2 scripts broken down section by section and sentence by sentence with explanations of how each element works and why each word was placed in the script. Your trainees need to understand why they are using these words, why tonality matters, and the psychology behind the words. This emphasis on understanding *why* makes your training more effective in three ways:

- It demonstrates respect for the sales reps' intelligence and skill. You aren't talking down to them or treating them like robots. This immediately puts to bed some of the most common concerns reps have about scripts.
- Understanding how each piece of the script gets them closer to their goals makes it easier to commit the script to memory.
- They will be able to respond appropriately if they get an unexpected answer, explain concepts in different ways if the prospect asks for clarification, and get back on script if the prospect derails them. They will be *learning* the script, not simply memorizing and reciting it by rote.

Next, you'll need a collection of successful sales calls from the lab so the trainees can hear their coworkers staying on script from beginning to end, using rebuttals effectively, and closing a sale. You can introduce them to the Call Breakdown Sheets to help them review the call.

Sometimes, it's impossible to find a call that stayed perfectly on script word for word. That's okay. Hearing another rep navigate back onto script when they accidentally get off is very valuable in training. It reassures the trainees they will be able to use the scripts effectively without being perfect. It also drives home the point that the scripts are tools to keep them from getting stuck and make them more successful. Playing a sample call that has a variety of "dos" and "don'ts" can also give trainees an example of how call breakdowns and manager feedback will work in the new system.

Finally, you should choose one or two lab members who can describe their experiences and results in learning to use the scripts. They should be enthusiastic advocates for the system, and the bigger the change in their performance, the better.

TRAIN MANAGERS FIRST

At least a day or two before training day for the sales reps, the script master should schedule training for the sales managers. They need a head start to understanding all the ins and outs of how the scripts work so they can coach and manage the reps going forward. Getting the managers on board is more important than the reps being on board, so they must be brought into the script system and made aware that this system is the future of the company. They must understand that the new process will not be optional. They will need to keep their team on script, and they will be accountable for doing so.

Present the system as part of the company's vision for the future, and make sure they understand why it is necessary: the company needs to grow its revenue and become scalable. When the company grows, scales, and becomes more profitable, everyone wins. There will be room for more people to get promoted. There will be more investment into people and incentives. The script will make it easier for managers to do their jobs and help reps be successful.

That's the carrot. There's also a stick: make sure your sales managers are aware that this change comes from the top and is firmly decided. Having a future with the company means supporting the new system, period. You will rely on them to set the tone for their teams. They need to communicate unequivocally that this is a change for the better and explain why.

During and after training, sales reps are going to look to their managers for guidance and ask their opinions about the change. If a manager isn't completely bought in and enthusiastic about the new system, they'll seed doubt in the minds of their team. Their skepticism or lukewarm response can spread like wildfire and affect the whole sales floor.

Use the Lab as a Case Study

You'll teach the scripts to your managers in much the same way you'll teach them to the reps on training day. You'll give them the Why Scripts for both calls, with explanations of how each section works. You'll teach them how to use breakdown checklists to monitor and analyze calls. You'll let them listen to successful calls and go over the positive results the lab is producing.

Again, this should not take a lot of convincing. If your script master and your lab have produced high-quality scripts and are implementing them correctly, the results will speak for themselves. Smart managers will be eager to see the same results from their own teams and focus on learning how to use the scripts and coach their teams effectively.

The most powerful thing you can do to help managers get familiar with the new system is to bring them into the lab while it's running. Let them shadow reps on the phone for Call 1 and Call 2, follow along with a copy of the script and a breakdown sheet, and see the scripts in action with real prospects.

Rules and Consequences

You must make sure your sales managers are equipped with strategies to coach reps who try to use the scripts and fail, as well as for dealing with those who resist using the scripts at all. Managers need to be in alignment about the rules for being on and off script and the ramifications for reps who are blatantly and persistently off process. It's reasonable to give reps a grace period of a month or so to get acclimated and adjust their habits.

After that, we recommend a progressive series of warnings, infractions, coachings, and (if necessary) termination. Managers must hold reps accountable for staying on script and working hard to improve. There's no room for debate, and the process cannot be optional.

This system is not a good fit for people who have trouble following directions and sticking with a program. Precise, consistent execution will produce amazing results. Spotty or sloppy execution will accomplish nothing. Going off script is contagious. If one person is allowed to drift off script without being corrected, eventually everyone will drift off with them, and the system will collapse. Managers must be prepared to coach people up or coach them out.

After the rollout, when the reps have seen how effective the scripts are, top performers tend to come on board. Ambitious, effective sellers can understand why the scripts work and how they benefit them. If a real outlier was already outperforming their peers by large margins (like our sales team's equivalent of basketball legend Michael Jordan, who was doing triple the sales of the next-highest performer), a manager can afford to give them some leeway about deviating from the scripts. Ask them to work with them, but it's not a good use of time to micromanage an outlier. Managers need to pick their battles.

More often, it's a few mediocre or underperforming reps

who resist using the scripts after rollout and complain they don't like or need them. Managers should shut that kind of attitude down firmly. Compliance with the company's processes is not optional. It's a fundamental job requirement. Once that rep becomes consistent and is performing at a very high level, they *might* earn some flexibility. But they must get on process and show results first.

Changes to the Manager's Role

The company must also prepare for the sales manager role to change. Many companies overcomplicate the manager role. They may have sales managers conducting job interviews, participating in marketing meetings, tracking payroll and commissions, doing administrative work, or running company-level meetings. We strongly recommend restructuring the role of sales manager to relieve them of those unrelated responsibilities.

Sales managers should spend 90 percent of their time overseeing and coaching their sales reps and maybe 5 percent on one-on-ones with their own supervisor and *nothing else*. They aren't business owners. They own their sales team. They own what their reps say on the phone. They own their team's performance. They should be in charge of attendance, performance, and their reps' growth. That's it. We even recommend that disciplinary actions be dealt with by more-senior leaders because it's time-consuming. Managers need to be on the sales floor, monitoring their team all day long.

Listening to calls, live coaching, and reviewing call breakdowns with reps are the lifeblood of this system. If a manager is giving enough feedback and help to each rep—individually, in small groups of reps with similar problems, or with the team as a whole—they won't have time for a bunch of administrative work. Upper management must support these permanent structural changes, and managers need to be trained and prepared for this shift in their workload and expectations.

> We'll take a deeper look at training managers to work within the new system in Chapter 8.

BUILD ANTICIPATION

The rollout should be cause for excitement. Once your training day is on the schedule, it needs to be hyped up so everyone can look forward to finding out all about the new system and seeing their results grow.

Training day is an all-day event, so if it's in person, plan to offer breakfast, plenty of coffee, a catered lunch, and snacks. If it's remote, you can give the reps a gift card to have their favorite lunch delivered. Your trainees need to be energized and paying attention. This system is supposed to help them succeed, so they should feel like they're being treated well. Plan to make it a fun experience, with music, giveaways, and a variety of activities. Make it special.

TRAINING DAY

Your training day needs to be planned and organized with the same care you put into creating the scripts. There's a logical progression of how to present the information. You also need to be mindful of the trainees' attention and energy levels so you can maximize learning. Schedule a ten-minute break every two hours (plus lunch, of course). Make sure to pass out copies of the agenda so the trainees can always know where they are, keep track of what they're learning, and plan around their personal needs. You should also record the training so anyone who couldn't be present can still learn what they need to know.

KICKOFF

The first thirty to forty-five minutes of your day will be devoted to introducing the system and the company's plans for the future. Typically, the intro is presented by the CEO, CRO, VP of sales, or senior figure leading the initiative.

They should explain why the new script system is the way forward for the company, pivotal to the company's success, and an absolutely necessary component of the trainees' jobs from this moment on. Together with the script master, they'll present the KPI results from the sales lab and project how the new system will lift up the reps' compensation. This intro should be positive, be motivating, and generate even more excitement for the trainees to jump into learning.

One thing to note is that the script master, like any teacher or trainer, must manage their classroom. You don't want anyone tuned out or falling asleep when they should be paying attention. The script master should make sure at the beginning of the training that everyone has a notebook and pen handy. The senior keynote speaker might even encourage the reps, at the very beginning, to take notes throughout the presentation.

You should also tell the trainees that you will have question-and-answer sessions regularly throughout the day, so they should hold their questions until then. There's a lot of material to get through, and it will probably answer most of the questions they have. If not, you'll address them all at once.

Holding questions will streamline the training and encourage the trainees to use their notepads.

Sometimes it helps to mention that the sales managers are observing the training, and they will note anyone who isn't appropriately attentive and address it with them after the session. You might even have to resort to calling on someone who's nodding off. That's awkward and confrontational, but you must make it clear this material is a big deal for the company, and it's very important they learn it. You're only going to hold this training once.

CALL 1 SCRIPT

From there, you'll present the Why Script for the initial cold call. As you saw in Chapters 1 and 2, a detailed explanation of the first script can get very granular. You'll review all the possible scenarios and objections prospects might throw at them.

Those scenarios should include type A, B, and F Prospects—along with instructions on how to respond to each of them. Many reps are relieved to learn that some prospects just can't be sold (and aren't worth the trouble). It takes a lot of pressure off them and helps them use their time better. However, most people forget this lesson after a hard day of being hung up on a lot. They need constant reminding—memories get short when people's emotions come into play.

Next, you'll play one or two example calls showing the script in action. Encourage the trainees to follow along with the script in their hands so they can hear the correct tonality for each segment and imagine themselves delivering the script the same way. Tonality can be the hardest part of a script to learn, so don't spend time trying to teach tonality during training day. Introduce the concept, and plan for the managers to do follow-up training and coaching once the reps have mastered reading and understanding the whys of the script.

Finally, you'll review the objections and rebuttals you identified for Call 1 and then have a question-and-answer session. By then, it's usually time for a break.

CALL 2 SCRIPT

When you come back from break, before launching into the Why Script for Call 2, it can be helpful to bring up one of your lab members to talk about their experiences with learning and using the scripts. They can discuss what areas they struggled with, how long it took them to feel like they'd mastered it, and how it improved their performance.

The Why Script for the demo call is much longer than the first script, with many more ways that a prospect might pull the rep off track. Going over every aspect of Call 2 is going to take up a significant portion of the day. As with any long training, the script master should plan to switch up the energy in the room and reinforce the material with a variety of games, group activities, and role-plays with volunteers.

After walking through all the elements of the Why Script, you should build in another question-and-answer period. Then you'll play a sample call. A successful demo call will typically be forty-five minutes or longer, plus you'll need time to stop and analyze it as you go. So you won't have time to play multiple sample calls as you did for Call 1. Just choose one very strong, successful demo so the trainees can hear how the rep uses their tonality, builds their relationship with the prospect, and ultimately closes the sale.

At the end of reviewing Call 2, you'll take questions one last time. If there's time left in the day, you can have the trainees break up into teams and practice delivering both scripts by role-playing different scenarios. Make sure you end the day on a high note, with plenty of encouragement and enthusiasm for their upcoming success with the new method. When the trainees hear how much confidence the script master, the lab members, and the senior leadership all have in the method—and particularly when they see the performance results—they should wind up looking forward to this new approach.

MAKING THE TRAINING STICK

Training doesn't end when the training day is over. Reps should continue to role-play in teams and develop the habit of deliberate practice on a daily and weekly basis. Most of that deliberate practice should be reviewing and analyzing actual calls using the call breakdown guides (reread the best practices in Chapter 5 or go on our website to download the Call Breakdown Sheets). Encourage them to use the call breakdown checklist on their own.

HARD CASES

After training day, managers may encounter different reactions from some of their team members. No matter how exciting or thorough the training might have been, some people will have a harder time adopting the new method. There may be isolated pockets of resistance or a negative attitude, and some reps may continue to struggle. Managers should deal with these issues promptly. They need to diagnose the root of the problem so they can address it in the most appropriate way.

Snipers

In the first week or so after rollout, managers should pull their teams off the floor for the last thirty minutes of the day to debrief (just like the sales lab's daily check-in). While the team is talking about how their day went and how the scripts are flowing for them, it's not unusual for one rep or another to get into a negative spiral. They may have had a frustrating day on the phones and blame the scripts for all the times they got hung up on or encountered an F Prospect. We call these reps "snipers" because they target the leader and disrupt the cohesion and morale of the squad.

If you recall, back in Chapter 4, we discussed the importance of challenging the prospect's thinking to stop a negative spiral. Managers should use the same techniques here and reassure the rep they'll address their concerns and help them work through trouble spots one-on-one. But you have to shut down and redirect the sniping so the meeting can maintain a positive focus. You don't want to set a precedent for the rest of the team to start griping about normal challenges. That will kill the momentum of the rollout.

The manager doesn't need anyone's approval to stick to the process. The process was rolled out because it has already proven its merit and been adopted by the company as a whole. They need to provide coaching and keep the team's focus on growing their skills and celebrating successes.

Slow Learners

People learn at different rates. That's inevitable. Every team will have some reps—veterans or new hires—who pick up the knack of using scripts in a few days or the first couple weeks. Other team members might take two to three months to get up to speed. What we've seen is about a quarter of your sales floor will pick up everything you're explaining right away and be ready to move on. The second quarter will get the gist of it and understand that it makes sense in general, but they might miss a few details. The third group doesn't get it, and they know they don't get it. They need you to explain it a different way, maybe multiple times. And the bottom quarter is totally off. There's no connection with the material at all.

These initial divisions in the learning curve do *not* dictate which reps are going to wind up being your best performers. Far from it. Sometimes a rep might take two months for the learning to sink in, but if they have a positive attitude and really want to improve, they wind up outperforming the quick studies. A fast learner might not have the patience and consistency to flourish in this system, while a slow-and-steady learner who is constantly trying to improve will wind up having a "lightbulb moment" sooner or later when it all comes together. Then they'll really start to shine.

It's obvious when a rep is trying their best and determined to make progress. Managers should work on keeping their spirits high and offering encouragement that it's normal to experience a learning curve. At the same time, they must give the rep actionable feedback on what they can do to get better. Reps need repetition on the phones, but they also need specific direction. If they just keep practicing wrong, they'll build wrong habits. They'll also lose hope that these thousands of repetitions will ever make a difference.

Managers need to consistently work with the slower learners to review their calls and point out particular areas where they were on and off script and what they should do differently next time. Then they need to follow up and make sure the rep is implementing the feedback.

Well-Intentioned "Helpers"

You want your reps to take ownership of the scripts and think about how they can improve their work. Unfortunately, for some people, that crosses over into thinking about how they can tweak and improve the script with their brilliant ideas. Sometimes reps and managers are very eager to make suggestions to the script master. Sometimes managers will tolerate reps routinely going off script or even encourage their team to rewrite their own version.

They mean well and truly want to help, but you cannot allow this kind of free-range scripting. The whole purpose of rolling out our system is to establish a single consistent standard across the board. If every team or every rep produces their personalized take on the script, you're back to square one, with improvisational selling or weak guidelines on how to run a call. Managers must understand the rules of keeping their reps on script and hold them accountable—or they are not suited to be managers at all.

Well-intentioned suggestions should be handled more delicately. It's true that the scripts will require updates in the long term. The product will get new releases and features. The marketing department may design better visuals or change the company branding. The script master might hear a rep make a great new rebuttal to a prospect objection that hasn't come up before. Or the competition might come out with a new product or feature that you need to address.

However, these script updates should be few and far between—several months apart, at least. Every change must be tested and approved by the script master before it gets accepted into the scripts. New ideas should be collected and combined into a single draft to minimize disruption. Frequent changes undermine the importance of being on script. After all, how can you be consistent if the scripts are different every week?

You don't want people focused on making continual suggestions to improve the scripts. They need to stay focused on executing the scripts they have and improving their own performance. At the same time, you don't want to tell enthusiastic reps or managers that you aren't interested in their ideas. That's going to crush their morale. It's best to collect all suggestions and let people know that their ideas will be reviewed, and when it's time to make an update, they'll be considered.

THE MAINTENANCE PHASE

We'll address more ways to support learning and address problems in Chapter 8. As you move forward from rollout, sustaining the best possible results from your new system will require you to implement best practices for hiring, onboarding, and management—and some of those practices may surprise you.

MANAGING YOUR NEW SALES SYSTEM

If you've followed the playbook so far, you've built an incredibly powerful sales machine. The way to keep that machine running indefinitely is to hire the right team members, train them correctly, and apply sound management principles to keep everyone on track. Now, this playbook isn't a primer on sales leadership or business management. There are plenty of those books—good ones—on the market already. In this chapter, we'll focus on specific aspects of team development within our system that are distinct from standard management practices. We'll cover:

- What attributes to watch out for in your hiring process (and what to look for)
- Profiles of reps who surprised everyone with their success in the system
- How onboarding new hires is similar to training in rollout and how it's different

- How to train managers for the system
- Best practices to manage reps within the system

HIRING

The standard mindset in hiring for traditional sales teams can often bring exactly the wrong results for our system. Typically, hiring managers look for impressive résumés, natural talent, and track records with a lot of experience. We've discussed from several different angles how experience in improvisational or relational selling doesn't really translate to our method. It often means a rep has a lot of habits they have to unlearn. The more success they've had selling their own way, the more resistant they'll probably be to doing it our way. That doesn't mean all successful, experienced reps won't work well in this environment—it just means they're more likely to struggle. To put it simply, we'll take a hardworking, positive, and coachable candidate with no sales background any day over someone with tons of sales experience and talent but who won't cooperate with and contribute to a scripted team and environment.

There's another aspect you should consider as well—résumés are easy to embellish. A candidate might claim all kinds of results, but we'd have no idea how to evaluate those claims. What was their part in achieving those results? Is the claim even accurate? And, of course, the most obvious question: if they have so much experience, why are they applying for an entry-level position?

A résumé can be useful to see if a candidate graduated and has a degree and to look for a lot of job-hopping or unexplained gaps in employment. Short stints at many different companies can be a red flag that the person quit or was let go quickly. Neither is a good sign.

You also have to trust your impressions of a candidate from the interview. Do their responses indicate they might oversell or outright lie to a prospect to get a sale? That's completely opposed to our philosophy. Are they genuine and sincere in their answers, or does your gut tell you they're a fake? There are many scenario-based questions that can help get a candidate to open up and show their attitude and personality.

QUALITIES TO LOOK FOR

The number one truth we've learned in developing this system is that talent is overrated. As we've mentioned, sales reps with lots of experience have very little advantage in a tightly scripted system, and the advantages they might have are outweighed by the temperament that usually comes as part of the package. As we discussed in Chapter 7, sellers who rely on charisma and improvisation tend to chafe at the structure of a script. If you already have talented outliers on your team who are willing to support and coexist with the new system, you can always find a place for them to contribute. But as you hire for the future, you aren't going to be on a talent search. You'll be on a character search.

In Chapter 6, we looked at the "the big three" qualities that make a good sales lab member: having a positive attitude, being a hard worker, and being coachable and open to feedback. "The big three" are also the main traits you should seek out when hiring new sales reps for the long term. They all work synergistically and are amplifiers for success within a scripted environment. So if the new hire you're interviewing signals all three traits, we highly recommend considering them for an opportunity at your organization. Here are some sample interview questions to ask for each of "the big three" to get you started:

Positive Attitude

- How do you handle feedback from customers, prospects, colleagues, or supervisors, particularly when it's not entirely positive?
- How do you handle rejection and setbacks in a sales environment? Can you give an example of a challenging situation and how you stayed positive throughout?
- Describe a situation where you faced a difficult prospect or client. How did you manage the interaction, and what steps did you take to ensure a positive outcome? What about a difficult team member or coworker? How did you handle the situation, and what did you learn from it?
- What do you find most rewarding about working in sales, and how does it contribute to your positive attitude in your role?
- Have you ever faced a situation where you didn't achieve your sales target? How did you react, and what actions did you take to improve?

Hard Worker

- What's the hardest thing you've ever worked on?
- Can you describe a time when you had to put in extra effort or work long hours to complete a project or meet a deadline? How did you manage your workload during that time?
- Can you share an example of a time when you took the initiative to go above and beyond your regular responsibilities to achieve a positive outcome?

Coachable

- How do you feel about a sales environment where reading a script is one of the responsibilities?
- How do you balance your own ideas and experiences with the guidance provided by your sales manager or team?
- Can you describe a time in your life when you received constructive feedback from a manager or mentor? How did you respond to that feedback, and what changes did you make to improve your performance?

Beyond "the big three," there are two other traits we recommend you look out for in potential new hires: competitiveness and natural communication skills.

Competitiveness is often overlooked as a desirable trait in hiring. A lot of people assume highly competitive candidates will be egotistical, but that's not necessarily true. Competitive people will push themselves to excel and be their best, but that doesn't mean they're divas who just want all the attention and glory for themselves. They want to be part of a winning team, and they'll do what it takes to help their team succeed.

Natural communication skills—When we're interviewing, there are some candidates who just have "it." What's "it"? They have great active listening skills, and they speak clearly and concisely and with great tonality. They build great rapport and have natural confidence. Those are the types of people you want in your organization (as long as they also signal they have "the big three"). In contrast, there are those who can almost be ruled out immediately. They sound unenthusiastic or lacking in passion. They might not be able to answer questions and convey their thoughts in an assured, coherent manner. They might ramble, go off on tangents, or lose their train of thought easily. If they can't sound excited and confident and get to the point quickly when they're selling themselves in a job interview, there's very little chance they could do it on the phone. We recommend moving on from them as quickly as possible.

SEE THEM IN ACTION

You should always make it clear early on in the interview process that the role is in a scripted environment and take time to ensure the candidates understand what that means. If your reps normally work on video and multiscreen with Power-Point, let candidates experience that and see how they handle it. Your interview process should include opportunities for the candidates to read and role-play a simplified version of your script (with proprietary information removed, of course), hear recorded calls, and shadow reps who are working on script and provide them a realistic expectation of how many dials they'll be making and types of conversations they'll be having each day.

This allows the candidates to experience the demands of the role and decide if they're able and willing to operate that way. It also allows you to see how they approach the script. If you give them a few minutes (or even days) to prepare, do they study and practice it? When it's time to role-play, do they actually follow the script at all?

The candidate's reactions to the scripted system will tell you a lot about whether or not they're a good fit. If they obviously have reservations about scripting, it might be too hard to retrain them. If they're glad to have the structure and follow directions, they're likely to be a better fit.

ONBOARDING

Once you've hired a new rep (or a class of new reps), you need to onboard them into the system. Some of the content they need to learn will be identical to the content used during your rollout training, and you can reuse those materials and concepts. However, new hires are coming into your company completely fresh. Before they can work with your scripts effectively, they need a base of knowledge.

When you plan and structure your onboarding, remember that you can't train everything all at once. We've seen too many trainers dump an information overload on brand-new hires. They can't take it all in. They wind up confused and don't retain anything.

You must prioritize the material your new hire needs to know first so they can build on their knowledge in a logical way. For example, you wouldn't train on tonality before you present the Why Script. You can't teach the why of the script before they understand your prospect's needs and your industry standards. And you can't expect them to sound like a product expert on the phone if they aren't even sure what your product does. Everyone has to "fake it till they make it" a little bit when they're new, but the less they have to fake, the better.

The first couple days of onboarding should focus on the basics. Start with your company's identity, principles, and values. Then you can introduce the fundamentals of your industry and your product. After that, you can present the Why Script, have them shadow another rep on the phones, and practice role-playing.

The next step would be to put them on the phones for a little while, followed by some time reviewing calls. This is a good time to introduce them to your breakdown checklist so they can see the skills they need to master and begin to set goals for themselves.

Overall, be mindful of the fact that your trainees proba-bly have little or no sales background. You'll have to prepare them for the experience of being on the phones so they don't get blindsided. They need to understand the three prospect types so they can put those various responses into context. You should give them reasonable expectations for their start-ing performance and learning curve. And they must be trained on how to handle rejection and keep themselves motivated throughout the day.

RAMPING UP

Learning to run demos is far more complicated than learning the Call 1 script. Delivering an effective demo requires technical savvy and the ability to multitask at a much higher level. You can help your new hires acclimate and use their training time productively by splitting their role during their ramp-up period.

Even if you don't normally split the SDR function from the account executive function, let your new hires function as SDRs for the first month or six weeks and hand off their demos to a more experienced rep. The extra practice will let them build expertise with the Call 1 script while they learn and practice the Call 2 script off the phones.

A demo script will contain at least thirty minutes of mate-rial, not counting any back-and-forth conversation with the prospect. Each element of the Call 2 Why Script builds on what came before. The reps need to understand which doors they are closing and how to incorporate prospect information, like goals and pain points, into the presentation. They also need to master tonality and be able to deliver the demo with a smooth flow. After that, they can begin running their own demos.

Again, we recommend allowing new reps time to acclimate

to the demo before giving them responsibility for objection handling and closing. Encourage them to run demos with business owners who are willing to listen, even if they know the prospect isn't in a position to buy. They need to practice navigating the slides, the software demo, and other technical aspects of the presentation.

Have them hand off closing to a manager at first. Then, as they get more comfortable with rebuttals, they can start closing with live coaching in their ear. Gradually, the manager can let them be more and more independent at closing, only chiming in if they're going in the wrong direction. Eventually, they'll get into the same routine as the other reps, requiring less monitoring.

There's an art to giving new reps the support they need to learn without making them overly dependent on the manager to close all their deals. What we call "baby-bird syndrome" is a real trap for both reps and managers. If you see reps ask for the sale and automatically turn to the manager to feed them lines like a baby bird waiting for its mother to drop it a worm, the manager needs to pull back and let them start handling things on their own. Sometimes the manager even needs to let them fail—like a mother bird kicking her baby out of the nest to teach it to fly.

Some prospects are just hard sells. They might need to hear from the manager as an authority figure or a second voice to validate what they've already heard from the rep. There will always be some need for managers to take over the occasional closing or make some follow-up calls. But managers can't get so focused on making every sale in the short term that they sacrifice a rep's long-term growth. Learning requires a balance between success and failure. Too much failure and the trainee will lose confidence. Too much support and they won't learn at all. Just like in school, a student making a solid B average is being challenged and working hard to succeed.

The manager's role in ramping up new hires is a great example of best practices for managing their team. We believe sales managers should be fully focused on coaching and developing their people into strong performers and future leaders.

MANAGING IN THE SCRIPT SYSTEM

In Chapters 6 and 7, we covered various aspects of managing reps in a scripted process, especially the importance of call reviews, detailed coaching, and accountability. There are a few more principles and techniques we recommend for sales managers that may reflect a different approach than they are used to in a traditional sales environment.

The best process and the best training in the world won't achieve lasting results if they're implemented as a one-time push with no follow-up. Over time, people have a tendency to drift back into old habits and fall off process—it's just human nature. Managers need to follow clear guidelines to make sure their teams execute the process (speed, tone, script theory, and active listening) correctly and consistently, day in and day out. Consistency is the key to everything we do, and we have a few tips that will help you create the right environment to execute on your new scripting.

The first key concept tied to good execution is the idea that 90 percent of a leader's time should be focused on coaching to process. Having a standardized scripting tool will not move the needle on the productivity of your team if you do not marry it to a coaching system or leadership playbook. Having the right playbook for your sales leaders to coach from can accelerate the success of your script and unlock the full potential of your team.

In our experience, the first step to spending 90 percent of your time coaching to process is understanding which reps you need to coach and what you should be coaching to. To do that effectively, you will need access to the right level of data. The modern-day sales leader is often bogged down in data and may have to access multiple software tools to understand one data trend. This is not only time-consuming but equally soul-crushing because it prevents the leader from doing the thing they need to be committed to: coaching to process. The solution is having one software tool that is your single source of coaching truth. How to find the right tool or stack for your sales team lies within what they need, but it should include the following:

- Call recording
- Full funnel data transparency
- CRM
- Sequencing functionality
- Dialer
- Lead routing

Once you have the software in place to tell you which reps to coach and KPIs to coach to, you need to implement your "Sales Leadership Philosophy" to guide the leaders on where and how to spend 90 percent of their time. A common trap sales leaders fall into is that once they have access to data, they begin "coaching" to everything and everyone. The reality is if you are coaching to everything, you are actually coaching to nothing and watering down your coaching value.

There is a more organized structure that enables the leader to be most effective by using what we call an "Impact Plan." The concept is very simple. On Monday morning by nine o'clock, the sales leader needs a game plan that dictates which reps they should be spending their time with that week in order to help those reps hit their pace targets. Let's start with the concept of pace. If the manager has a target of $20,000 monthly recurring revenue (MRR) and there are twenty selling days in the month, then by Friday of the first week, the first five days will have elapsed. In that case, the leader needs to be at 25 percent to pace by the end of the week (which is $5,000 of MRR). Once that has been established, the leader can begin building his or her Impact Plan to achieve that goal. Less is more when creating your Impact Plan. The idea is to have a template you can fill in and update every week to help you focus. Items we have found successful to building an Impact Plan are:

1. Identify your pace gap. Identify what is in your pipeline and how many follow-up calls and/or decision calls you have for the week.
2. Identify which reps you need to spend time with.
3. Choose the single most impactful KPI to work on with each of these reps for that point in time.
4. Start small and only look at the main KPIs, like dials, decision maker rate, demo set rate, demo hold rate, and close rate.
5. Share your Impact Plan with your direct manager.

A very helpful tool that will complement your management of a scripted environment and give you directional guidance on your Impact Plan is the concept of the "End of Day Report."

The End of Day Report is a simple form you require each of your sales reps to complete by the end of the day and send out to sales leadership. The report consists of three sections:

1. Daily Metrics: This includes dials, demos set, demos held, and demos closed.
2. What Went Well: Here reps provide business names where the call went well and a link to the recorded call, if available. They should recap what specifically happened that went well and outline the next steps (e.g., if a demo is set, note the date and time).
3. Areas of Opportunity: Reps should recap what didn't go well for the day and identify areas of opportunity. This includes objections they're encountering and obstacles they're struggling with.

These reports are not only for the rep's benefit but also to assist everyone supporting the rep. Managers, coaches, and executives can quickly review KPIs to see if a rep had a good or bad day. However, KPIs alone often lack the context of *why* the rep performed well or poorly. The End of Day Report provides this context, saving time by highlighting the anecdotal issues reps face.

For example, if a rep made one hundred dials in a day but set no demos, the KPIs will indicate they are struggling with setting demos. Without context, the reason for this struggle is unclear. However, if the rep notes in "What Went Well" that they are successfully getting past gatekeepers but mentions in "Areas of Opportunity" that the decision maker keeps hanging up on them in the first twenty seconds of the call, you know you should likely be looking at decision maker intros when reviewing calls.

Using these End of Day Reports alongside tools like the Call Breakdown Sheet is the most effective way we've seen for reps (and managers) to stay on process.

The final concept that reinforces many of the points we listed above is that of *reflection*. Managing a sales goal can be very emotional, and if you are managing eight to ten reps who also carry the weight of a sales goal, that can compound both the emotional load of the job and the quality of your impact. From our experience, the final bookend to managing within the scripted environment is the idea of using Friday afternoon as an opportunity to reflect on what happened during the week. This is not your time to build your Impact Plan for the next week and set up your next pace goal. Think of this as your meditation time to go deeper into general observations about what you accomplished during the week and, more importantly, what you learned as you attempted to hit your pace goal. We often see that what the leader learns through this period of reflection is more important than the work they did because what they learned will inform their next Impact Plan. The need for learning is a feature most managers take for granted, along with the need for self-improvement and personal development. Reflection can happen in the form of self-sent voice notes, journaling, or simple note-taking. Reflection also helps you practice the idea of balance and ensure you are spending enough time away from work and sales goals. Time away from work is therapeutic and will give you, as the team leader, needed perspective on your work. This perspective is often hard to see in the heat of the emotion of your job.

Good examples of things you can practice to achieve balance in your life are:

1. Leave your phone on your nightstand for one day during the weekend and detach from Slack.
2. Read non-business-related articles or books.

3. Connect with friends and family, and practice being present with them in the moment.
4. Develop your nonwork interests.
5. Exercise.

The broader point here is an important one: you are only as good a leader as you allow yourself to be. And like anything, balance is your window to own your own potential. Managing within a scripted environment requires focus, dedication, and commitment. And to be your best during the workweek, you need time away to reflect before the clock resets at 9:00 a.m. on Monday.

FROM THEORY TO ACTION

All the stages of your Sales Lab Scripting system are complete. You've researched, constructed, and tested your custom scripts. You've documented and shared your results. You've replicated the system on every level of your sales operation. You've proved that the science of scripting works, and now you can reap the benefits: satisfied prospects, happy customers, predictable (and unstoppable) sales growth, powerful training and coaching, a world of options in hiring, and a healthy, sustainable culture for everyone in your organization.

CONCLUSION

We're passionate about the power of scripting. Can you tell?

Lots of people can teach how to sell products and services over the phone. We do it better.

We believe there are all sorts of entrepreneurs out there who have products that could change the world for the better but haven't yet cracked the code on selling them at a high level. We wrote out the code for you.

We believe this system has an unprecedented ability to drive your company's growth, scale your sales operations, transform your culture, and empower individual reps, managers, and leaders within your organization. It will help you create a successful, predictable, replicable, scalable sales process from beginning to end.

We hope reading this book made a believer out of you.

If you're ready to dive deeper into the art and science of scripting, you can find a wealth of resources on our website, www.Sellfire.com/SalesLabScripting:

- Downloadable templates that will help you write your own customized scripts
- Virtual trainings on our philosophy and techniques
- Monthly webinars and group coaching calls
- Multimedia samples of correct tonality for different sections of a script
- Call breakdown checklists and other coaching tools
- Resources to help you plan and organize your own sales lab or rollout

Need more hands-on help from a dedicated script master? We recommend you contact the team at Sellfire.com. Sellfire helps companies, teams, and individuals maximize their impact through a purpose-built, complete solution for high-velocity sales.

If you learned something from this playbook—even one strategy that will improve your work—follow us on social media and let us know! Better yet, let other people know. Give a copy of this book to your VP of sales. Recommend it to people in your network. There's someone you know who needs this playbook, and the success they achieve with it will put them in your debt.

So it's time to ask the important questions. Of all the things you've read in this book, is there anything that makes you think our system wouldn't be a good fit for your business? Would you say our system is better than what you're doing now?

If you've reached this point in the book and you're still reading, it's clear you have the drive to be an expert at what you do. Maybe you started a company with the hope of making millions and changing your industry. Maybe you're looking for a successful exit that will give you more freedom in life. Maybe you're looking to build a sales career. Whatever the dream, if you have a truly great product, there's no reason you shouldn't be selling enough and scaling enough to realize those dreams. This is a proven world-class playbook, and we challenge you to take what you have learned and put it into action.

ACKNOWLEDGMENTS

Stephen Defina—Words cannot fully express our gratitude for your tireless dedication to this project. You were more than a contributor; you were a cocaptain, and we are endlessly thankful for your support and hard work.

To Dave Rubin, Matt Stuart, and Drew Johnson—Thank you for believing in us, investing in our success, and helping make this dream a reality.

Ellen Seltz, Darnah Merciecah, Ellie Cole, and rest of the Scribe team (past and present)—Your hard work and dedication turned this book into something we are incredibly proud of. It was a roller-coaster ride, but your commitment helped us cross the finish line, and for that, we are deeply grateful.

Jessica Ruvalcava—Your creative vision brought our book cover to life. Thank you for translating our ideas into something so impactful.

We also extend our heartfelt thanks to the following individuals for their invaluable feedback and guidance during the writing process:

Ben Rubenstein

Branick Weix

Angela Dunham

Chris Heller

John Berkowitz

Tom Calvert

Finally, to all the employees and companies we've had the privilege of working with—Your hard work and dedication on the phones inspired the stories and lessons shared in these pages. Without you, this book would not exist.

www.ingramcontent.com/pod-product-compliance
Lightning Source LLC
Chambersburg PA
CBHW030505210326
41597CB00013B/801